Presented to:

_____

By:

_____

Date:

_____

WATER FROM THE ROCK

AFRICAN-AMERICAN EDITION

TIMELESS WRITINGS TO STRENGTHEN YOUR FAITH
AND ANCHOR YOUR SOUL

HONOR HB BOOKS

Inspiration and Motivation for the Seasons of Life

COOK COMMUNICATIONS MINISTRIES
Colorado Springs, Colorado • Paris, Ontario
KINGSWAY COMMUNICATIONS LTD
Eastbourne, England

Honor Books® is an imprint of
Cook Communications Ministries, Colorado Springs, CO 80918
Cook Communications, Paris, Ontario
Kingsway Communications Ltd., Eastbourne, England

Water from the Rock: African-American Edition—Timeless Writings to
Strengthen Your Faith and Anchor Your Soul
© 2005 BORDON BOOKS

First printing, 2005
Printed in Canada
3 4 5 6 7 Printing / Year 09 08 07 06 05

Developed by Bordon Books
Manuscript written by Niral Burnett
Designed by Koechel Peterson and Associates

Scripture quotations marked KJV are taken from the King James Version of
the Bible; NIV are taken from the Holy Bible, New International Version
NIV®. Copyright © 1973, 1978, 1984 by International Bible Society.
Used by permission of Zondervan Publishing House. All rights reserved;
ASV are taken from the American Standard Version. Copyright © 1901 by
Thomas Nelson & Sons and copyright © 1929 by International Council
of Religious Education; NRSV are taken from the New Revised Standard
Version of the Bible, copyright © 1989 by The Division of Christian
Education of the National Council of the Churches of Christ in the USA.
Used by permission. All rights reserved; NASB are taken from the New
American Standard Bible. Copyright © The Lockman Foundation 1960,
1962, 1963, 1968, 1971, 1972, 1973, 1975, 1977, 1995. Used by per-
mission.

Antiquated spellings, vocabulary, and punctuation usage in the selected
texts of some of the historical writers quoted in this book have been edited to conform to present-day American English usage so that the edited
quotations will convey the same meaning to the contemporary reader that
the original writers intended to express.

ISBN: 1-56292-355-2

*W*ATER FROM THE ROCK
AFRICAN-AMERICAN EDITION

TIMELESS WRITINGS TO STRENGTHEN YOUR FAITH
AND ANCHOR YOUR SOUL

TABLE OF CONTENTS

INTRODUCTION

Water from the Rock: African-American Edition—Timeless Writings to Strengthen Your Faith and Anchor Your Soul is a devotional filled with the writings of great men and women of God—writings we believe will offer you wisdom and insight as you strive to live as a Christian in this world. It also includes entries that are specific to the needs of African Americans, written or spoken by historic African-American figures.

We pray that your faith will be strengthened and your heart encouraged as you read excerpts from the teachings of such great Christians as Booker T. Washington, Martin Luther King Jr., Charles Haddon Spurgeon, Frederick Douglass, Hannah Whitall Smith, John Wesley, and so many more. These timeless insights of well-known—and some not-so-well-known—classic Christian writers will leave you better equipped to live in harmony with your Creator. And like water from a rock in the midst of the desert, these pages are sure to refresh your thirsty soul.

[God] split the rocks in the desert and gave them water as abundant as the seas; he brought streams out of a rocky crag and made water flow down like rivers.

PSALM 78:15-16 NIV

To Seek, to Feel, and to Find

[God] hath made of one blood all nations of men for to dwell on all the face of the earth, and hath determined the times before appointed, and the bounds of their habitation; that they should seek the Lord, if haply they might feel after him, and find him, though he be not far from every one of us.

ACTS 17:26-27 KJV

God created mankind to dwell on all the face of the earth and predetermined exactly where they would live. Every ethnicity has the eyes of God looking upon it, waiting for each one to fulfill His purpose. That includes you. There was a purpose behind the arrival of your ancestors to the very nation in which you stand. According to the verse above, that purpose was, and continues to be, to seek the Lord.

In a world that has grown increasingly complex with all of its demands, we have to wonder what we could do without the hand of God to guide us through our lives. How could we arrive safely to the end of every day without the protective and loving hand of our Father to lead us? The Scripture tells us that we are to "feel after Him, and find Him."

No matter how challenging life may seem, it is good to know that God has placed us exactly where we are, for His purpose—to seek after Him, to feel after Him, and to find Him. He wants us to seek after Him while He stands near, waiting for us to embrace His love and care for us. He wants us to feel after Him during those especially rough times when it seems as if He is absent. God desires that we find Him, so He assures us that He is not far from any one of us.

We will always have the assurance of His promises to us, no matter where we find ourselves in life. All God desires of us is that we seek after Him with our whole hearts. This is our purpose—to seek, to feel, and to find.

BREATHE FORTH LOVE

I say then, Walk in the Spirit, and ye shall not fulfill the lust of the flesh.

GALATIANS 5:16 KJV

A spiritual walk is the most beloved walk of all in the sight of God. But it is easy for us to miss His pleading that we fellowship with Him. To walk in His presence is like soliciting the company of an old friend, who longs for your love and your presence. He stands there, watching and hoping that you will approach. Then when you do, you have fulfilled His joy because you have put your affection on Him.

O crucified Jesus in whom I live, and without whom I die; mortify in me all sensual desires, inflame my heart with thy holy love, that I may no longer esteem the vanities of this world, but place my affections entirely on thee.

Let my last breath, when my soul shall leave my body, breathe forth love to thee, my God; I entered into life without acknowledging thee, let me therefore finish it in loving thee; O let the last act of life be love, remembering that God is love.

-Richard Allen

Have you given your life to God? Doing so goes beyond

reciting a prayer and going to church services every so often. Is your life so committed that you cannot think anything outside placing your affections entirely on Him? Truly, to live in such a way is to have given your life to Him. Such a life is also the expectation of the believer.

If you have not truly given Him your life, perhaps today is the day to refresh and rekindle the flame that once existed in your heart. You can approach Him just as you are, and He will be there, waiting for you with open arms.

There are commands in the Bible to love God, but truly, God is committed to loving you even more. No matter what sin you have committed, and how far gone from His presence you may feel, He longs to hear from you today, and He will have the same longing tomorrow and forever. Go boldly into His presence today, and He will make you clean and pure, never desiring to be separated from you again.

THE LORD, OUR REFUGE

Because thou hast made the Lord, which is my refuge, even the most High, thy habitation; there shall no evil befall thee, neither shall any plague come nigh thy dwelling.

PSALM 91:9-10 KJV

Today's world has ushered in unthinkable challenges to humankind. There are wars, famine, moral decay, and sorrow before our eyes every day. Clearly, this world is in a lot of pain, and the temptation to worry is, for many, a constant companion. Yet, our refuge and habitation is in God. His promises tell us that the evil of this world shall not befall us.

Have you ever faced a time in life where it seemed that you were surrounded by overwhelming opposition? Has it ever seemed that during such times, God was absent? The good news is, He was never absent. He was always there, loving you and waiting for your arrival into His presence. He continually desires that you walk with Him daily. He wants to be your refuge.

In one of his many great sermons, the great preacher of the 1800s George Whitfield (1714-1770) said: "Now you find more pleasure in walking with God one hour than in all your former carnal delights and all the pleasures of sin. O! the joy you feel in your own souls, which all the men of the world and all the devils in hell, though they were to combine together, could not destroy."

Walking with God is what defines the life of the true believer. It does not matter how great the torment of this world or the challenges of your life; God is your refuge and is able to help you overcome anything that comes your way. All of the adversity of our lives, combined into one, cannot be compared to one mere hour with our Father in Heaven.

George Whitfield walked with God. He was committed to God in such a way that the poet, scholar, and slave, Phyllis Wheatley (1753-1784), wrote of his death:

> *He prayed that grace in ev'ry heart might dwell,*
> *He longed to see America excel;*
> *He charged its youth that ev'ry grace divine*
> *Should with full lustre in their conduct shine;*
> *That Saviour, which his soul did first receive,*
> *The greatest gift that even a God can give,*
> *He freely offered to the num'rous throng,*
> *That on his lips with list'ning pleasure hung.*
>
> *But, though arrested by the hand of death,*
> *Whitfield no more exerts his laboring breath,*
> *Yet let us view him in the eternal skies,*
> *Let ev'ry heart to this bright vision rise;*
> *While the tomb safe retains its sacred trust,*
> *Till life divine re-animates his dust.*

-PHYLLIS WHEATLEY

God Is for You

What shall we then say to these things? If God be for us, who can be against us?

Romans 8:31 KJV

"One and God make a majority."

This simple, yet profoundly true statement was penned by one of the greatest abolitionists in American history, Frederick Douglass (1818-1895). Yet, he often had to spend his own life as one, alone in a cause where it seemed that the odds were constantly against him. It was during these lonely times that he learned the necessity of faith in God.

From my earliest recollection, I date the entertainment of a deep conviction that slavery would not always be able to hold me within its foul embrace; and in the darkest hours of my career in slavery, this living word of faith and spirit of hope departed not from me, but remained like ministering angels to cheer me through the gloom. This good spirit was from God, and to Him I offer thanksgiving and praise.

-Frederick Douglass

There is a mark on the horizons on all of our lives, that

when passed, will offer a prize that comes from God. Our job as Christians is to hold fast to the living word of faith. We are to stay our course in the path that God has chosen for us, and by no means are we to lose hope.

God is indeed for us. And this truth leaves the adversary without options. You will be triumphant. The glorious declaration in the book of Jude sums up for us an eternal victory, when it tells us:

"Now unto him that is able to keep you from falling, and to present you faultless before the presence of his glory with exceeding joy, to the only wise God our Saviour, be glory and majesty, dominion and power, both now and ever. Amen" (vs. 24-25 KJV).

In the "living word of faith," God has promised a magnificent ending for all who walk with Him. The life of Frederick Douglass ended with freedom. This former slave went on to become a prolific writer, an abolitionist, and a United States ambassador. What is in store for you, if you choose to walk in the path God has chosen for you? What will soon happen if you allow Him to continually work in your favor, starting today? Who can be against you if God is for you? You and God make a majority.

THE JOY OF A GOOD CONSCIENCE

Seeing we have this ministry, as we have received mercy, we faint not; but have renounced the hidden things of dishonesty, not walking in craftiness, nor handling the word of God deceitfully; but by manifestation of the truth commending ourselves to every man's conscience in the sight of God.

2 CORINTHIANS 4:1-2 KJV

The glory of a good man is the testimony of a good conscience. Therefore, keep your conscience good and you will always enjoy happiness, for a good conscience can bear a great deal and can bring joy even in the midst of adversity. But an evil conscience is ever restive and fearful. Sweet shall be your rest if your heart does not reproach you.

To glory in adversity is not hard for the man who loves, for this is to glory in the cross of the Lord. But the glory given or received of men is short-lived, and the glory of the world is ever companioned by sorrow. The glory of the good, however, is in their conscience and not in the lips of men, for the joy of the just is from God and in God, and their gladness is founded on truth.

He who minds neither praise nor blame possesses great peace of heart and, if his conscience is good, he will easily be contented and at peace.

Praise adds nothing to your holiness, nor does blame take anything from it. You are what you are, and you cannot be said to be better than you are in God's sight. If you consider well what you are within, you will not care what men say about you. They look to appearances but God looks to the heart. They consider the deed but God weighs the motive.

It is characteristic of a humble soul always to do good and to think little of itself. It is a mark of great purity and deep faith to look for no consolation in created things. The man who desires no justification from without has clearly entrusted himself to God: "For not he who commendeth himself is approved," says St. Paul, "but he whom God commendeth."

-THOMAS À KEMPIS
THE IMITATION OF CHRIST

THROUGH THE EYES OF GRACE

By grace are ye saved through faith; and that not of yourselves: it is the gift of God: Not of works, lest any man should boast.

EPHESIANS 2:8-9 KJV

Who do you see when you look in the mirror? Do you see a person who has seen a life of success? Do you see imperfection and need? Perhaps you see a person who is striving to live an honest life and to be the best person he or she can be. No matter how you view yourself, God sees you as a person whose actions in the past have little resemblance to who you are now. No matter what you have done in the past, all of your sins are washed away forever, if you belong to Him. You are clean and free—forever separated from the darkness of the past. God now looks upon you through the eyes of grace—not of your own actions, good or bad. When we place our faith in Him to save us from sin, He does not take into account our past works. He takes into account only the combining of our faith and His amazing grace.

There was a young captain of a slave-ship whose life made such grace necessary. For part of his life, this man, John Newton (1725-1807), had seen and committed countless atrocities against his African captors. He was especially known for his violent temper and his blasphemy. He was even known by the other sailors, who themselves were of vile reputation, as little more than an animal. Yet, it was a violent storm that served as the turning point in John Newton's life.

Calling this storm his "great deliverance," Newton says it was here that the saving power of God became real to him. During this storm, he came face-to-face with a need for a Savior. His simple prayer, "Lord, have mercy upon us," was the beginning of his new life in Christ. Surviving the storm, he clearly knew that it was not only his ship and crew that were saved, but also his soul.

John Newton was forgiven and saved because of the grace of God. By the same grace, our sins are also forgiven. No matter what the sin, God's grace is great enough to forgive us for them all. Even once we have known Christ, His grace is available to us, in case we find ourselves fallen into willful sin. The Bible says, "If we confess our sins, he is faithful and just to forgive us our sins, and to cleanse us from all unrighteousness" (1 John 1:9 KJV).

There is no sin too great or state too low for God to forgive and restore. His great love, by which He loved us upon the cross at Calvary, has brought salvation to all who call upon His name. Have you found yourself fallen in a sea of torments? Has your own wrongdoing put you in a place where it seems all will be lost? The simple prayer, "Lord, have mercy upon us," can bring the saving grace you need today, just as it did for the young captain of a slave-ship.

The repentant heart of John Newton resulted in more than two hundred hymns, one of which became one of the most well-known and best loved of all—"Amazing Grace." Later in his life, he continued to preach the Gospel and even began to speak out against the slave trade. Yet, it was his miraculous conversion at sea that meant the most to him.

In a Puritan sermon called *One Thing Needed*, John Newton wrote the following in order to describe the value of the grace he found:

One thing is needful: a humble, dependent spirit to renounce our own wills and give up ourselves to His disposal without reserve. This is the path of peace and it is the path of safety, for He has said, the meek He will teach His way, and those who yield up themselves to Him He will guide with His eye. . . . Jesus is a complete Savior and we bring more honor to God by believing in His name and trusting His word of promise than we could do by a thousand outward works.

-JOHN NEWTON

Today, God sees this humble man of God, John Newton, through the eyes of grace. In this very same way, God looks upon you as a person covered by His grace. The next time you look in the mirror, gaze with an assurance in your heart that your sins have been washed away. There remains no work to do in order to please God. All that is left is to apply our saving faith, in order to receive God's amazing grace.

Speak Not Harshly

A soft answer turneth away wrath.

Proverbs 15:1 kjv

Have you ever had to work with a difficult person? It is not always easy to be around those you are not compatible with, but there is a way to handle these times, when other people try to get the best (or worst) of us.

Seldom can a heart be lonely
If it seeks a lonelier still,
Self forgetting,
Emptier cups with love to fill.

Speak not harshly—much of care
Every human heart must bear;
Enough of shadows darkly lie
Veiled within the sunniest eye.

By thy Childhood's gushing tears,
By thy griefs of after years;
By the anguish thou dost know,
Add not to another's woe.

Speak not harshly—much of sin
Dwelleth every heart within;
In its closely-covered cells,
Many a wayward passion dwells,

By the many hours misspent,
By thy gifts to errors lent,
By the wrong thou didst not shun
By the good thou hast not done,

With a lenient spirit scan
The errors of thy fellow man.

-JOANNA P. MOORE

There is no need to speak harshly to our fellow man when we have God on our side. We can still speak the truth, but we can do so in love. We can still confront, but we do not have to combat. We must remember that although others have faults in their lives, we are not perfect either. And God forgave us with a lenient spirit. He had unending mercy towards us. He loved us with an everlasting love. We can do the same for others, and the blessing of God can overflow in our lives because we have done so.

CREATION

God said, "Let us make man in our image, after our likeness: and let them have dominion over the fish of the sea, and over the fowl of the air, and over the cattle, and over all the earth, and over every creeping thing that creepeth upon the earth."

GENESIS 1:26 KJV

God made you for himself. In fact, creation was not perfect until He had created mankind. Can you bring even more glory to His day by spending time with Him? He is ready and willing to fellowship with you, anytime you are.

> *Then God walked around,*
> *And God looked around*
> *On all that He had made.*
> *He looked on His world*
> *With all its living things*
> *And God said: I'm lonely still.*
>
> *Then God sat down—*
> *On the side of a hill where He could think;*
> *By a deep, wide river He sat down;*
> *With His head in His hands,*
> *God thought and thought,*
> *Till He thought: I'll make me a man!*

Up from the bed of the river
God scooped the clay;
And by the bank of the river
He kneeled Him down;
And there the great God Almighty
Who lit the sun and fixed it in the sky
Who flung the stars to the most far corner of the
     night,
Who rounded the earth in the middle of His hand,
This Great God,
Like a mammy bending over her baby,
Kneeled down in the dust
Toiling over a lump of clay
Till He shaped it in His own image;

Then into it He blew the breath of life,
And man became a living soul.
Amen. Amen.

-JAMES WELDON JOHNSON

He created you just for this purpose—to be a soul alive to Him. You have the chance today to live in His presence continually. And He would be pleased to welcome you to himself.

THE MIND OF CHRIST

Let this mind be in you, which was also in Christ Jesus.

PHILIPPIANS 2:5 KJV

How should the Christian think? How should we respond to the issues in life that affect us? The classic author and hymnist John Wesley (1703-1791) gave a passionate discourse on this very subject, which speaks to us, even today:

Here is the sum of the perfect law, the circumcision of the heart. Let the spirit return to God that gave it, with the whole train of its affections. Other sacrifices from us He would not, but the living sacrifice of the heart hath He chosen. Let it be continually offered up to God through Christ, in flames of holy love. And let no creature be suffered to share with Him; for He is a jealous God. His throne will He not divide with another; He will reign without a rival. Be no design, no desire admitted there, but what has Him for its ultimate object. This is the way wherein those children of God once walked, who being dead still speak to us: "Desire not to live but to praise His name; let all your thoughts, words, and works tend to His glory." "Let your soul be filled with so entire a love to Him that you may love nothing but for His sake." "Have a pure intention of heart, a steadfast regard to His glory in all your actions." For then, and not till then, is that "mind in us, which was also in Christ Jesus," when in every motion of our heart, in every word of our tongue, in every work of our hands, we 'pursue nothing but in relation to Him, and in subordination to His pleasure"; when we, too, neither think nor speak nor act to fulfil "our own will, but the will of Him that sent us;" when, "whether we eat or drink, or whatever we do," we do it all "to the glory of God."

-JOHN WESLEY

STEAL AWAY TO JESUS

[Jesus said,] "Come unto me, all ye that labour and are heavy laden,
and I will give you rest."

MATTHEW 11:28 KJV

There is nothing more refreshing than fellowship with
God. Yet, this is the very thing that is most neglected in the
life of the Christian. A multitude of reasons exist as to why so
many rarely take the time to go to God in prayer. However,
such excuses pale in comparison to the life-situations of the
man and slave, Thomas Lewis Johnson (1836-?). At his conversion, he immediately learned the value of prayer in his personal life. In his memoirs, he testifies of his experience:

After my conversion I would often "steal away to Jesus"
with other slaves to some quiet place for prayer—over the stable or in the kitchen when the master and mistress were away,
though we knew that if we were discovered we should be
locked up for the night and that the next morning we should
receive from five to nine or even thirty lashes for unlawfully
assembling together.

Over five slaves in such a gathering, though they had passes, constituted an unlawful assembly. At night no slave was
allowed to be out without a pass from his master. We used to

have such a good time at these meetings. No wonder the Jubilee Singers sang with such deep feeling when those of them who were once slaves remembered the meetings of this kind at which they sang and prayed almost in a whisper for fear of being heard. How appropriate to sing softly and quietly:

> *Steal away,*
> *Steal away,*
> *Steal away to Jesus;*
> *Steal away,*
> *Steal away home;*
> *I ain't got long to stay here.*

-THOMAS LEWIS JOHNSON

Is there anything in your life that can stop you from "stealing away" to Jesus? Can any hardship or pain draw you away from just one sustained embrace in the bosom of your Father in Heaven? Had you committed a sin in every moment of every day past, there would still be more than enough grace, more than enough love, more than enough power to keep you in all your ways, if only you would steal away to Jesus.

'Go, and I Will Go with You'

*[The Lord says,] "Ask of me, and I will make the nations your
inheritance, the ends of the earth your possession."*

PSALM 2:8 NIV

Have you ever faced a time in life when you wondered if
you were really fulfilling the reason you were born? From the
beginning of creation, this quest has been in the center of the
hearts of individuals worldwide. Yet in the lives of many people, this purpose is never fulfilled, and consequently, every day,
a potentially world-changing destiny ends in the grave of some
unwilling soul. How do we discover such a great destiny?
What do we do in order to begin fullfilling the reason we were
born? The nineteenth century "colored evangelist" Amanda
Smith (1837-1915) knew very well what she had to do. We
also must do the same.

As the Lord led, I followed, and one day as I was praying
and asking Him to teach me what to do, I was impressed that
I was to leave New York and go out. I did not know where, so
it troubled me, and I asked the Lord for light, and He gave me
these words: "Go, and I will go with you."

-AMANDA SMITH

33

As the Lord led, she followed. But how did she know the Lord led? She knew through prayer. She knew through knowing God. The calling of an evangelist missionary led this former slave girl to England, Ireland, Scotland, India, and Africa. Where will your calling lead you? Today, ask of God, and He will bring the nations before you, not as an inheritance of earthly gain, but of heavenly opportunity. Even if you are not a missionary to foreign lands, there is no mission that is beyond the scope of prayer. You can seek the face of God as innumerable souls stand in the balance. Those souls remain lost, waiting for you to begin to walk in all for which God has made you. Some of them are right in your neighborhood. Will you answer His call? Will you ask of Him? If you go, He will go with you.

TRIFLE NOT YOUR TIME AWAY

Saith [Jesus] unto his disciples, "The harvest truly is plenteous, but the labourers are few; pray ye therefore the Lord of the harvest, that he will send forth labourers into his harvest."

MATTHEW 9:37-38 KJV

How much time do we really have? Have you ever noticed that as a child, years took a long time to pass? But as you got older, the years seemed to go by as if they were months. Seeing this pattern, we do not have as much time as we think, because time goes by as the wind, and you can never get it back once it blows past. What will you do with the time you have today? The harvest is waiting for you.

> *Ye ministers that are called to preaching,*
> *Teachers and exhorters too,*
> *Awake! Behold your harvest wasting;*
> *Arise! There is no rest for you.*
>
> *To think upon that strict commandment*
> *That God has on his teachers laid:*
> *The sinners' blood, who die unwarned,*
> *Shall fall upon their shepherd's head.*

35

But, O dear brethren, let's be doing—
Behold the nations in distress;
The Lord of hosts forbid their ruin,
Before the day of grace is past.

We read of wars and great commotions,
Before the great and dreadful day:
Oh! Sinners, turn your sinful courses,
And trifle not your time away.

But oh! Dear sinners, that's not all that's dreadful;
You must before your God appear,
To give an account of your transactions,
And how you spent your time when here.

-RICHARD ALLEN

There is no more time to lose. God wants us totally and fully, every day. If you give your limited time to Him on earth, He has a glorious eternity waiting for you.

PERFECT REST

There remaineth therefore a rest to the people of God.

HEBREWS 4:9 KJV

How different will be the state of the believer in Heaven from what it is here! Here he is born to toil and suffer weariness, but in the land of the immortal, fatigue is never known. Anxious to serve his Master, he finds his strength unequal to his zeal: his constant cry is, "Help me to serve Thee, O my God." If he be thoroughly active, he will have much labour; not too much for his will, but more than enough for his power, so that he will cry out, "I am not wearied of the labour, but I am wearied in it." Ah! Christian, the hot day of weariness lasts not for ever; the sun is nearing the horizon; it shall rise again with a brighter day than thou hast ever seen upon a land where they serve God day and night, and yet rest from their labours.

Here, rest is but partial, there, it is perfect. Here, the Christian is always unsettled; he feels that he has not yet attained. There, all are at rest; they have attained the summit of the mountain; they have ascended to the bosom of their God. Higher they cannot go. Ah, toil-worn labourer, only think when thou shalt rest for ever! Canst thou conceive it? It is a rest eternal; a rest that "remaineth." Here, my best joys bear "mortal" on their brow; my fair flowers fade; my dainty cups are drained to dregs; my sweetest birds fall before Death's arrows; my most pleasant days are shadowed into nights; and the flood-tides of my bliss subside into ebbs of sorrow; but there, everything is immortal; the harp abides unrusted, the crown unwithered, the eye undimmed, the voice unfaltering, the heart unwavering, and the immortal being is wholly absorbed in infinite delight. Happy day! Happy! When mortality shall be swallowed up of life, and the Eternal Sabbath shall begin.

-CHARLES HADDON SPURGEON

LOOKING AT YOUR BEST

The communication of thy faith may become effectual by the acknowledging of every good thing which is in you in Christ Jesus.

PHILEMON 6 KJV

There are few in the world who trouble us as often as the person we look at in the mirror every day. Our experiences in life bring us to a place where we know ourselves better than we would like. However, in God's eyes, there are good things inside of us. Sadly, we so often view the bad things that it is easy to become blinded to the good things that are inside of us. The conversion story of this nineteenth-century slave tells us how we should begin to see ourselves when we belong to Christ:

At last, I gave myself up to the Lord, to do what He would with me, for I was a great sinner. I began to see the offended justice of God. O! my readers, the anguish of my heart! I thought the whole world was on me, and I must die and be lost.

In the midst of my troubles, I felt that if God would have mercy on me, I should never sin again. When I had come to this, I felt my guilt give way and thought that I was a new being. Now, instead of looking with my real eyes to see my

Savior, I felt Him in me and I was happy. The eyes of my mind were open, and I saw things as I never did before. With my mind's eye, I could see my Redeemer hanging upon the cross for me.

-THOMAS JONES

Thomas Jones acknowledged something good inside himself. Then, no matter what he had to face, no matter what issues confronted him, he saw the goodness of Christ living in him.

What do you see when you look within? Do you see a wretched sinner, or do you see someone redeemed by Jesus Christ? Our faith is made effectual, or effective, when we begin to see ourselves as God desires and acknowledge every good thing He has put inside us.

WHAT HAVE YOU BEEN DOING?

According to my earnest expectation and my hope,
that in nothing I shall be ashamed, but that with all boldness,
as always, so now also Christ shall be magnified in my body,
whether it be by life, or by death.

PHILIPPIANS 1:20 KJV

We all desire certainty in this uncertain world. But often, our desire for peace and safety can be the enemy of our spiritual lives. An African-American minister by the name of Reverend Lott Cary (1790-1828) understood the cost of giving all for Christ when he became one of the first African-American missionaries to Africa. His story tells us a great deal of what it means to truly be committed to Christ, regardless of all the world tries to offer us.

He seemed to have imbibed the sentiment of Paul and to have great heaviness and continual sorrow in his heart for his brethren, his kinsmen according to the flesh.

At the close of his farewell sermon in the First Baptist Meeting House in Richmond, he remarked in substance, as follows:

I am about to leave you and expect to see your faces no more. I long to preach to the poor Africans the way of life and salvation. I don't know what may befall me, whether I may find a grave in the ocean, or among the savage men, or more savage wild beasts on the Coast of Africa; nor am I anxious what may become of me. I feel it my duty to go, and I very much fear that many of those who preach the Gospel in this country will blush when the Saviour calls them to give an account of their labors in His cause and tells them, "I commanded you to go into all the world and preach the Gospel to every creature."

Then with the most forcible emphasis he exclaimed:

The Saviour may ask, "Where have you been? What have you been doing? Have you endeavored to the utmost of your ability to fulfil the commands I gave you, or have you sought your own gratification and your own ease, regardless of My commands?"

-REVEREND LOTT CARY

Have we all sought our own, rather than the things of Christ? Let the story of Lott Cary speak volumes to your spirit. Most of all, let the love of Christ compel you to go where you have never gone before, and commit yourself to do His will.

My Soul, What Canst Thou Give

How can I repay the Lord for all his goodness to me? I will lift up the cup of salvation and call on the name of the Lord.

PSALM 116:12-13 NIV

What shall we render? What can we give to a God who has given us everything? He that spared not His own Son, how can we ever repay?

> *For mercies, countless as the sands,*
> *Which daily I receive*
> *From Jesus, my Redeemer's hands,*
> *My soul what canst thou give?*
> *Alas! From such a heart as mine,*
> *What can I bring him forth?*
> *My best is stained and dyed with sin,*
> *My all is nothing worth.*
> *Yet this acknowledgment I'll make*
> *For all he has bestowed;*
> *Salvation's sacred cup I'll take*
> *And call upon my God.*
> *The best returns for one like me,*
> *So wretched and so poor;*

Is from his gifts to draw a plea,
And ask him still for more.
I cannot serve him as I ought,
No works have I to boast;
Yet would I glory in the thought
That I shall owe him most.

-JOHN NEWTON

Jesus gave His life for us, so it is only a reasonable service to give our lives to Him. It is only fair to lay our lives before God and dedicate ourselves to glorifying Him. Then, after a lifetime of glorious service to God, we will realize in His everlasting presence, that we could never pay Him back for all He has done. Not because we have done too little, but because through His lovingkindness, He has given too much.

FROM TEARS TO JOY

*Although the fig tree shall not blossom, neither shall fruit be
in the vines; the labour of the olive shall fail, and the fields shall yield
no meat; the flock shall be cut off from the fold, and there shall be
no herd in the stalls: Yet I will rejoice in the Lord, I will joy in
the God of my salvation.*

HABAKKUK 3:17-18 KJV

What though I mourn and am afflicted here, and sigh
under the miseries of this world for a time, I am sure that my
tears shall one day be turned into joy, and that joy none shall
take from me. Whoever hopes for the great things in this
world takes pains to attain them; how can my hopes of everlasting life be well ground, if I do not strive and labor for that
eternal inheritance? I will never refuse the meanest labors,
while I look to receive such glorious wages; I will never repine
at any temporal loss, while I expect to gain such eternal
rewards.

Blessed hope! Be my chief delight in life, and then I shall
be steadfast and immovable, always abounding in the work of
the Lord, be my comfort and support at the hour of death,
and then I shall contentedly leave this world, as a captive that
is released from his imprisonment.

-RICHARD ALLEN

LET YOUR SOUL BE PREPARED

How shall we escape, if we neglect so great salvation.

HEBREWS 2:3 KJV

Today, are you conscious of the reality that God is looking upon you? He loves you and desires His best for your life. Do you love Him and desire to give Him your best? Moreover, is your soul prepared for an eternity with Him?

There is an urgency that exists in the soul of every man and woman on earth to be in right standing with God. John B. Meachum (1789-1854) was well aware of that urgency and gave his life to feverently preach to those who would hear his voice declaring for them to get right with God.

O, do not let the judgment find the soul unprepared! Feet, where are you carrying the soul to? Are you not walking in forbidden paths? Death may be in some of these paths. Hands, how often have you warred against the soul, doing the very thing that God hath forbidden? Mouth, have you not helped to damn the soul, by cursing and swearing and lying?

All these things lead down to the pit of damnation. Eyes, what are you about, that you cannot watch for the soul, and not suffer these feet and hands and mouth to do so much mischief to the soul? because, if you do not watch these many members, they will damn the soul to all eternity. It seems that the tongue is an unruly member; James says, "it cannot be tamed; it is unruly, and full of deadly poison; set on fire of hell." Cannot the eye watch the other members, and keep them from damning the soul, by running headlong into forbidden paths? I condemn all the members, eye, hand and foot; they are all agreed together, to go on and war against the soul. Then the mind must be changed. God keep thy tongue from evil and thy lips from speaking guile.

It is out of the abundance of the heart that the mouth speaketh, and with the heart men believe unto righteousness, and with the mouth confession is made unto salvation. These things do not war against the soul; you have fruit unto holiness, and the end is everlasting life. How much better, then, it is to endeavor to save the soul!

Let all seek to have the mind changed, that we may be led by the Spirit of Christ. In order to be led by the Spirit of Christ, we must be born again; born of that Spirit that can lead us from earth to that blessed world of rest, that remains for the people of God.

Come, friends, don't read. Do no more. You must make the inquiry, how stands the case between God Almighty and your soul; and endeavor to receive the Spirit of Christ, that you may be a lively stone in the building, meet for the Master's use, cleansed by His blood! A lively stone in the building? We must live godly and soberly in Christ Jesus the Lord, which is your salvation.

-JOHN B. MEACHUM

Be Still My Heart

Be still, and know that I am God.

PSALM 46:10 KJV

Be still my heart! These anxious cares
To thee are burdens, thorns, and snares,
They cast dishonor on thy Lord,
And contradict his gracious word!
Brought safely by his hand thus far,
Why wilt thou now give place to fear?
How canst thou want if he provide,
Or lose thy way with such a guide?
When first before his mercy-seat,
Thou didst to him thy all commit;
He gave thee warrant, from that hour,
To trust his wisdom, love, and pow'r.
Did ever trouble yet befall,
And he refuse to hear thy call?
And has he not his promise past,
That thou shalt overcome at last?

-JOHN NEWTON

Sometimes, the hardest thing to do when troubles surround us is to be still. We are often tempted to try to find our own way of solving the problems that arise. Doing so often gets us into worse situations.

During our search for answers, God stands, waiting for us to call upon Him. It is at the point of calling Him that our efforts cease and His efforts begin. How can we lose faith with God as our guide? How can we ever be cast down?

Sometimes, all of the joy that we ought to walk in is wasted in needless worry. As the hymn says, "Oh, what peace we often forfeit, oh, what needless pain we bear. All because we do not carry everything to God in prayer."

Cast your cares upon Him and be thankful to Him. Do not fret or worry about what will happen tomorrow. God holds all of our tomorrows and will take care of us in due season. We are obliged only to walk in His joy and trust in Him.

HE'LL MAKE IT PLAIN SOMEDAY

Although the fig tree shall not blossom, neither shall fruit be in the vines; the labour of the olive shall fail, and the fields shall yield no meat; the flock shall be cut off from the fold, and there shall be no herd in the stalls: Yet I will rejoice in the Lord, I will joy in the God of my salvation. The Lord God is my strength, and he will make my feet like hinds' feet, and he will make me to walk upon mine high places.

HABAKKUK 3:17-19 KJV

One of the hardest things to handle in the Christian life is to be confronted with prayer that seems unanswered. After laboring and seeking the face of God for days, months, and even years, it is never an easy thing to rest content when it seems that Heaven has not heard you. What do we say to the person who faces such apparent contradiction? What do we say to ourselves when all seems lost and Heaven is silent? The old Negro spiritual says it well:

> *Though many a time no signs appear,*
> *Of answer when I pray;*
> *My Jesus says I need not fear,*
> *He'll make it plain someday.*
> *I'll be like Him someday,*
> *I'll be like Him someday;*

My Jesus says I need not fear,
He'll make it plain someday.

He'll make it plain one day. All of the questions we have in this world will be answered in the life to come. Someday, we will see Jesus as He is, and we will see ourselves glorified and shining in His image. In that day, we will understand the unanswerable, and will learn why this Christian walk was well worth the while. Until then, we have the honor of rejoicing in the God of our salvation. He is the strength we need in order to live as victors in this world. And even when it looks as though we are surrounded by darkness, He will cause our spirits to soar to new heights every day.

LOVE THAT OBEYS

We beseech you, brethren, and exhort you by the Lord Jesus,
that as ye have received of us how ye ought to walk and to
please God, so ye would abound more and more.

1 THESSALONIANS 4:1 KJV

The word "obey" brings about thoughts of submission and compliance to the will of another—things that we almost never enjoy doing, when it comes to mankind. But obedience to God is always for our own good. Obedience to God is His instruction to us for a more fulfilling life. If we choose to do what He says, we will be able to experience our life on this earth to the fullest. His will is our roadmap to blessing.

Whoever loves, desires to please the beloved object; and according to the degree of love is the greatness of desire; make me O God diligent and earnest in pleasing thee; let me cheerfully discharge the most painful and costly duties; and forsake friends, riches, ease and life itself, rather than disobey thee.

Whoever loves, desires the welfare and happiness of the beloved object; but thou, O dear Jesus, can'st receive no addition from my imperfect services; what shall I do to express my affection towards thee? I will relieve the necessities of my poor brethren, who are members of thy body; for he that loveth not his brother whom he has seen, how can he love God whom he hath not seen?

-RICHARD ALLEN

What more can we give except our obedience to Him? For even the words of our mouth and the praise of our lips mean little if not coupled with our submission to Him. Yes, whosoever loves, desires to please the beloved object. Here and now, our beloved is our Lord. Can we love Him today? Can we obey? It is always for our own good.

SOLD TO THE HIGHEST BIDDER!

*Present your bodies a living sacrifice, holy, acceptable unto God,
which is your reasonable service. And be not conformed to
this world: but be ye transformed by the renewing of your mind,
that ye may prove what is that good, and acceptable,
and perfect, will of God.*

ROMANS 12:1-2 KJV

We have all heard the tragic stories of young men and
women of long ago who were forced to stand upon auction
blocks, waiting to be sold to the highest bidder. Against their
will, they were humiliated publicly and forced under the own-
ership of the one who purchased them. A life of servitude
mixed with pain and suffering was almost always certain to
follow.

The scenario we speak of describes the history of the
American slave trade. Yet, it also describes the life of the
Christian who is enslaved by the things of this world. Being
controlled by the adversary, such a Christian stands, waiting
for a new enemy to take control of his or her life and master
it. This person, too, will not have much more to expect than a
life of servitude, pain, and suffering. A redeemer is needed in a
life such as this. Therefore, God came to earth, in the person
of Jesus Christ, to fulfill such a need.

Today, there is no auction block to stand upon. Jesus

Christ redeemed us from a spiritual auction block over two thousand years ago by experiencing, himself, the agony of the cross. If we would present ourselves to Christ, rather than to that which seeks to enslave us, we will attain unspeakable freedom. No longer will we have to suffer the humiliation and taunting that comes from the fruit of our sins. The freedom of our reasonable service to God will cause us to live as free men and women, without the bondage of slavery to our adversary, the Devil. Jesus will stand as our advocate, having purchased our salvation in His own blood; and we will continue our lives in Him, in His love, in His liberty, by His faith—sold to the Highest Bidder.

CHOSEN, NOT CURSED

According as he hath chosen us in him before the foundation of the world, that we should be holy and without blame before him in love.

EPHESIANS 1:4 KJV

Before they would go their separate ways to replenish the earth, a disturbing occurrence happened in the life of Noah's sons that would change history forever—especially for the black race. Noah's son Ham committed a sin that brought a curse upon his descendants. According to Genesis 10, out of the descendants of Ham were those who went southward to dwell in Africa. Sadly, it is often said that these Africans were cursed by God when He declared, "Cursed be Canaan."

"He said, Cursed be Canaan; a servant of servants shall he be unto his brethren. And he said, Blessed be the Lord God of Shem; and Canaan shall be his servant. God shall enlarge Japheth, and he shall dwell in the tents of Shem; and Canaan shall be his servant" (Genesis 9:25-27 KJV).

Yet, it was only the descendants of this one son of Ham who were cursed. Ham had three other sons who were not cursed and were presumably of the same race as their father. (See Genesis 10:6.) Notwithstanding, the mercies of God are great, and the curse upon the Canaanites did not last through all generations. This becomes clear when we read the list of the disciples of our Lord Jesus Christ:

"Simon he surnamed Peter; and James the son of Zebedee, and John the brother of James; and he surnamed them Boanerges, which is, The sons of thunder: And Andrew, and Philip, and Bartholomew, and Matthew, and Thomas, and James the son of Alphaeus, and Thaddaeus, and Simon the Canaanite." (See Mark 3:16-18.)

The Genesis account of the curse upon the descendants of Canaan was often used to justify slavery. Yet, the last apostle listed in our Holy Bible was Simon the Canaanite. He was a descendant of Canaan. But he was not cursed. Neither was he a slave. Chosen by God as an apostle, he unashamedly proclaimed the Gospel. According to church tradition, in the end, he died the same death as our Lord, crucified for doing the will of God. How great is the mercy and love of our Lord that He would establish His Church through those once cursed!

There is no curse upon the black race. Anyone can be redeemed, never to be cursed again, if we call upon the name of the Lord Jesus. Today, remember that you are the chosen and the blessed—the Christian.

MAKING BLACK HISTORY

*Brethren, I count not myself to have apprehended: but this one thing
I do, forgetting those things which are behind, and reaching forth
unto those things which are before.*

PHILIPPIANS 3:13 KJV

The road ahead of us is glorious. But we have to let go of
the anger of the past. One of the hardest things to do in our
Christian life is to forget those things that are behind us.

> Stony the road we trod,
> Bitter the chastening rod,
> Felt in the days when hope unborn had died;
> Yet with a steady beat,
> Have not our weary feet
> Come to the place for which our fathers sighed?
> We have come over a way
> That with tears has been watered,
> We have come, treading our path
> Through the blood of the slaughtered,
> Out from the gloomy past,
> Till now we stand at last
> Where the white gleam of our bright star is cast.

-JAMES WELDON JOHNSON

The greatest view of Black America is the view of the future. Our mothers and fathers in times past did indeed "sigh" and long for the place we are today. And while the past was indeed gloomy, the future is glorious, and we owe thanks to God for such glory.

We also ought to be thankful and appreciative of the bravery and tears of the men and women who paved the way for us, people such as Harriet Tubman, Sojourner Truth, Frederick Douglass, Booker T. Washington, and countless unnamed people whom you will never hear of in history books. These are people who endured chains, survived torture, and labored tirelessly as slaves but in their hearts were servants only to Christ. The prayers of our mothers and fathers have brought us to where we are now.

Let us never, through an acceptance of mediocrity and immorality, allow their tears and prayers to be in vain. Let us make black history. Let us strive righteously to our glorious future, with Jesus Christ being our head. For, more than any other, we owe our gratitude to the One who made us free, not only from slavery, but from a world of sin.

WE'LL UNDERSTAND IT BETTER

It is written, Eye hath not seen, nor ear heard, neither have entered into the heart of man, the things which God hath prepared for them that love him.

1 CORINTHIANS 2:9 KJV

There are things that happen in life that we will never understand on this side. But there is another side, beyond this life, that will usher us into a place where all knowledge exists. There, we will understand the reason for everything we endured on this earth. And knowing where we will be in that day, it will be worth it all.

> We are tossed and driv'n on the restless sea of time;
> Somber skies and howling tempests oft succeed a
>   bright sunshine;
> In that land of perfect day, when the mists have rolled away,
> We will understand it better by and by.

> We are often destitute of the things that life demands,
> Want of food and want of shelter, thirsty hills and
>   barren lands;
> We are trusting in the Lord, and according to God's Word,
> We will understand it better by and by.

Trials dark on every hand, and we cannot understand
All the ways that God could lead us to that blessed
> *promised land;*
But He guides us with His eye, and we'll follow till we die,
For we'll understand it better by and by.

-CHARLES ALBERT TINDLEY

After the tears of this life, we will rest in the light of God's love, never to hurt again. God has prepared for every one of us something that our natural eyes and ears cannot comprehend. He has prepared for us the glory of His kingdom.

There is a place that awaits us where the brightness of His glory will never go dim; a place where those who were blind will see; where those who hurt are healed; where those who are suffering find rest—everlasting rest. This place awaits those who "follow till they die."

Are you that person who will follow Christ? Are you willing to walk with Him through the "thirsty hills and barren lands" that are so often crossed over in this journey of life? If so, there is no need to worry about the earthly things that so often try to take your focus off of God. Just determine to keep your eyes on Him. And in that great day—by and by—you will walk upon a land so great, all of the questions of this life will fade away as you gaze upon God's eternal glory.

GOODNESS AND PEACE IN MAN

If it be possible, as much as lieth in you, live peaceably with all men.

ROMANS 12:18 KJV

First, keep peace with yourself; then you will be able to bring peace to others. A peaceful man does more good than a learned man. Whereas a passionate man turns even good to evil and is quick to believe evil, the peaceful man, being good himself, turns all things to good.

The man who is at perfect ease is never suspicious, but the disturbed and discontented spirit is upset by many a suspicion. He neither rests himself nor permits others to do so. He often says what ought not to be said and leaves undone what ought to be done. He is concerned with the duties of others but neglects his own.

Direct your zeal, therefore, first upon yourself; then you may with justice exercise it upon those about you. You are well versed in coloring your own actions with excuses which you will not accept from others, though it would be more just to accuse yourself and excuse your brother. If you wish men to bear with you, you must bear with them. Behold, how far you are from true charity and humility which does not know how to be angry with anyone, or to be indignant save only against self!

It is no great thing to associate with the good and gentle, for such association is naturally pleasing. Everyone enjoys a peaceful life and prefers persons of congenial habits. But to be able to live at peace with harsh and perverse men, or with the undisciplined and those who irritate us, is a great grace, a praiseworthy and manly thing.

Some people live at peace with themselves and with their fellow men, but others are never at peace with themselves nor do they bring it to anyone else. These latter are a burden to everyone, but they are more of a burden to themselves. A few, finally, live at peace with themselves and try to restore it to others.

Now, all our peace in this life is found in humbly enduring. He who knows best how to suffer will enjoy the greater peace, because he is the conqueror of himself, the master of the world, a friend of Christ, and an heir of heaven.

-THOMAS À KEMPIS

MORE FRUIT

[Jesus said,] "Every branch that beareth fruit, he cleanseth it, that it may bear more fruit."

JOHN 15:2 ASV

The thought of fruit is so prominent in the eye of Him who sees things as they are, fruit is so truly the one thing God has set His heart upon, that our Lord, after having said that the branch that bears no fruit is taken away, at once adds: and where there is fruit, the one desire of the Husbandman is more fruit. As the gift of His grace, as the token of spiritual vigor, as the showing forth of the glory of God and of Christ, as the only way for satisfying the need of the world, God longs and fits for, more fruit.

More Fruit—This is a very searching word. As churches and individuals we are in danger of nothing so much as self-contentment. The secret spirit of Laodicea—we are rich and increased in goods and have need of nothing—may prevail where it is not suspected. The divine warning—poor and wretched and miserable—finds little response just where it is most needed.

Let us not rest content with the thought that we are tak-ing an equal share with others in the work that is being done or that men are satisfied with our efforts in Christ's service or even point to us as examples. Let our only desire be to know whether we are bearing all the fruit Christ is willing to give through us as living branches, in close and living union with himself, whether we are satisfying the loving heart of the great Husbandman, our Father in Heaven, in His desire for more fruit.

More Fruit—The word comes with divine authority to search and test our life: the true disciple will heartily surrender himself to its holy light and will earnestly ask that God himself may show what there may be lacking in the measure or the character of the fruit he bears. Do let us believe that the Word is meant to lead us on to a fuller experience of the Father's purpose of love, of Christ's fullness, and of the wonderful privilege of bearing much fruit in the salvation of men.

More Fruit—The word is a most encouraging one. Let us listen to it. It is just to the branch that is bearing fruit that the message comes: more fruit. God does not demand this as Pharaoh the task-master, or as Moses the lawgiver, without providing the means. He comes as a Father, who gives what He asks and works what He commands. He comes to us as the living branches of the living Vine and offers to work the more fruit in us, if we but yield ourselves into His hands. Shall we not admit the claim, accept the offer, and look to Him to work it in us?

-ANDREW MURRAY

TAKE HIM!

[Jesus saith,] "Behold, I stand at the door, and knock: if any man hear my voice, and open the door, I will come in to him, and will sup with him, and he with me."

REVELATION 3:20 KJV

The plea of Christ that we should listen to His voice holds within it such a great promise of glorious fellowship. Such a plea to one who does not know God is certainly eye-opening. But the plea of Christ, from behind the door of which He stands, is not directed to the sinner, but the believer. His call is to His beloved Church. It is to those who have allowed the cares of this life to overwhelm them so much that the fiery passion they once had for Him has lessened. God's heart's desire is for the Church to be drawn to Him again.

Does the passion in your heart still burn for God? Are your thoughts still consumed by the one who calls himself a "consuming fire?" Have you ever really sought God in such a way that there was no doubt in your mind that He was there with you at all times? If today you cannot say "yes, and amen" to any of these things, perhaps it is time to open yourself wide to Him once again. The offer still stands with our Lord, outside the doorway of your heart. Will you hear His voice and take Him? Will you open up your heart once again, fellow believer? Will you commit this day to a fresh commitment to God?

Take him ye starving sinners, for your food;
Ye thirsty, come to this life-giving stream,
Ye preachers, take him for your joyful theme;
Take him my dear Americans, he said,
Be your complaints on his kind bosom laid:
Take him, ye Africans, he longs for you,
Impartial Saviour is his title due:
Wash'd in the fountain of redeeming blood,
You shall be sons, and kings, and priests to God.

-PHYLLIS WHEATLEY

Phyllis Wheatley penned these words from the great preacher George Whitfield, many of which still resonate in the hearts of believers today. Perhaps it resonates in your heart right now. Will you take Him?

I BELIEVE

My son, forget not my law; but let thine heart keep my command-
ments: For length of days, and long life, and peace, shall they add to
thee. Let not mercy and truth forsake thee: bind them about thy
neck; write them upon the table of thine heart: So shalt thou find
favour and good understanding in the sight of God and man.

PROVERBS 3:1-4 KJV

To believe means to have a conviction that something is true. And Richard Allen knew well his conviction and passion for the one true God. He gave his life to serving a God he could not see, but in whom he believed. Let his words encourage you today:

I believe, that according to the types and prophecies which went before You, and according to Your own infallible prediction, You did by Your own power rise from the dead the third day, that You did ascend into Heaven, that there You sit on Your throne of glory adored by angels, and interceding for sinners.

I believe, that You have instituted and ordained holy mysteries as pledges of Your love, and for a continual commemoration of Your death; that You have not only given Yourself to die for me, but to be my spiritual food and sustenance in that holy sacrament, to my great and endless comfort. O may I frequently approach Your altar with humility and devotion, and work in me all those holy and Heavenly affections, which become the remembrance of a crucified Savior.

I believe, O Lord, that You have not abandoned me to the dim light of my own reason, to conduct me to happiness; but that You have revealed in the holy Scriptures whatever is necessary for me to believe and practice, in order to my eternal salvation.

O how noble and excellent are the precepts; how sublime and enlightening the truth; how persuasive and strong the motives; how powerful the assistances of Your holy religion, in which You have instructed me; my delight shall be in Your statutes, and I will not forget Your word.

I believe, it is my greatest honor and happiness to be Your disciple: how miserable and blind are those that live without God in the world, who despise the light of Your holy faith.

-RICHARD ALLEN

"I believe" is the statement that takes us out of the darkness of this world and into the glory of God's kingdom. Our belief in a faithful God opens the doors of blessing for us. In Him, we find favor. Knowing Him brings us into a journey that causes us to experience the best of life. Belief in Him brings us healing and prosperity in every area of our lives. Belief in Him assures us a glorious eternity in His presence. How wonderful it is that no matter what life brings, "I believe" is the declaration that can change everything for the better.

OUR BLESSED HOPE

The Lord himself shall descend from heaven with a shout, with the voice of the archangel, and with the trump of God: and the dead in Christ shall rise first: Then we which are alive and remain shall be caught up together with them in the clouds, to meet the Lord in the air: and so shall we ever be with the Lord.

1 THESSALONIANS 4:16-17 KJV

Either we will meet Him or He will meet us. But one thing is for certain—we shall be with Him someday. This is our blessed hope. This life offers us many challenges, trials, and more than a few temptations. Yet, the grace of our Lord assures us a place with Him if we put our trust in Him. It takes more than a vivid imagination to visualize that glorious day, but it is coming for us all. When we shall see Him as He is, it is certain that most of us will stand there speechless, gazing at the expressed image of God's perfect love. No trial or temptation on earth will be able to compare to that day.

> *Yea, when this flesh and heart shall fail,*
> *And mortal life shall cease,*
> *I shall possess, within the veil,*
> *A life of joy and peace.*
> *The earth shall soon dissolve like snow,*
> *The sun forbear to shine;*

But God, who called me here below,
Shall be forever mine.
When we've been there ten thousand years,
Bright shining as the sun,
We've no less days to sing God's praise
Than when we'd first begun.

-JOHN NEWTON

The classic song speaks of eternity with such longing and passion. But have you ever really thought about the future of the one who puts his or her trust in Jesus Christ? This glorious future is as real as this very moment. Life presents many challenges, and your plans for today may not all go the way you expect, but the great day of the Lord shall come, and you are going to be a part of it. So, be of good cheer! You have a blessed hope!

It's Not What You Know

*That I may know him, and the power of his resurrection, and the
fellowship of his sufferings, being made conformable unto his death.*

Philippians 3:10 KJV

"It's not what you know, but who you know."

We hear this phrase very often, especially when we are
looking for advancement in some area of our lives. But do you
know that this statement may have more truth to it than we
have acknowledged? Of all the things the apostle Paul had
achieved in his life, the thing he considered the single greatest
was his living relationship with God through Jesus Christ.
Consider his own words on the matter:

"What things were gain to me, those I counted loss for
Christ. Yea doubtless, and I count all things but loss for the
excellency of the knowledge of Christ Jesus my Lord: for
whom I have suffered the loss of all things, and do count
them but dung, that I may win Christ, And be found in him,
not having mine own righteousness, which is of the law, but
that which is through the faith of Christ, the righteousness
which is of God by faith" (Philippians 3:7-9 KJV).

All of the things he felt were beneficial to his earthly

walk—the career, the positions of authority, the notoriety of man—all of those things were counted as worthless so that he could know Christ. Because of his decision to know Christ, he was persecuted beyond anything most of us can imagine. But in the end, he fulfilled the purpose for which God had placed him on this earth. Two thousand years later, Paul's writings are still impacting lives every single day. Coupled with being an irreplaceable spiritual giant in Church history, he is known to be one of the most renowned intellectuals of all time. Paul lost a lot in his decision to follow Christ. Yet, through knowing Christ, he gained more than even he could have ever imagined.

What will you gain today if you make the decision to "know" Christ? Will you dare take your relationship with God beyond the week-by-week worship services, sermons, and traditions? Should you dare go beyond your life of predictability, where do you suppose God will take you? In the end, it is not what you know, it is who you know. And the one you need to know will take you where you desperately long to go. Such a daring question bears repeating: Will you know Him?

HIS BURDEN IS LIGHT

[Jesus said,] "Take my yoke upon you, and learn of me;
for I am meek and lowly in heart:
and ye shall find rest unto your souls.
For my yoke is easy, and my burden is light."

MATTHEW 11:29-30 KJV

God has provided us a way of escape from all of life's hardest times. That way out is Jesus. The days we face may seem rough, but most of us would not dare compare our light affliction with the pains of slavery. But one simple man, a former slave, was able to overcome the burdens of this life through the power of the cross.

The good old man had told me that the "Lord had great work for me to do," and I must prepare to do it; that he had been shown that I must preach the Gospel. His words made a very deep impression upon me, and I verily felt that some such work was before me, though I could not see how I could ever engage in its performance. "The good Lord would bring it to pass in his own good time," he said, and that I must go on reading and studying the Scriptures. This advice and these suggestions were not without their influence on my character and destiny. He fanned my already intense love of knowledge into a flame by assuring me that I was to be a useful man in the world. When I would say to him, "How can these things be?" and "What can I do?" his simple reply was, "Trust in the Lord." When I would tell him, "I am a slave, and a slave for life. How can I do anything?" he would quietly answer, "The Lord can make you free, my dear; all things are possible with Him; only have faith in God. 'Ask, and it shall be given you.' If you want liberty, ask the Lord for it in FAITH, and He will give it to you."

Thus assured and thus cheered on under the inspiration of hope, I worked and prayed with a light heart, believing that my life was under the guidance of a wisdom higher than my own. With all other blessings sought at the mercy seat, I always prayed that God would, of His great mercy, and in His own good time, deliver me from my bondage.

-FREDERICK DOUGLASS

Frederick Douglass received his redemption during a time when this earth offered nothing but bondage for a black man. And yes, God delivered him from his bondage. Yet, the bondage that needed to be broken was that bondage on the inside of his heart. He needed Jesus, first. He needed the heavy burden he carried to be placed upon Christ. In exchange, a calling was revealed to him that would forever change American history. He became a man of influence during the presidency of Abraham Lincoln. He strove greatly as an abolitionist crusader. And yes, he was a ferverent preacher of the Gospel. He exchanged the burden of his sins, his cares, his bondage, for the light burden of obeying God.

Today, the offer still stands for those who "labor and are heavy laden." Will you come to Christ? Will you exchange the cares of this world for His call? The decision is yours.

DO WE REALLY NEED HIM?

All we like sheep have gone astray; we have turned every one to his own way; and the Lord hath laid on him the iniquity of us all.

ISAIAH 53:6 KJV

More than anything we will ever need on this earth, we need Him. We need His grace and mercy. We need His love. The reason is that there does not exist a sinless person in this world. We have all, at some time or another, fallen into the trap of coming short of God's desire. However, when we humbly state that we need Him, do we really know what we are saying? We are declaring that we needed Christ to suffer; we needed Him to be beaten; we needed Him to dangle upon the cross at Calvary. We needed Him to die. Not only did we need Him to die for us, but God the Father needed Christ to die in order to redeem us from our sins. In fact, the scripture tells us that "it pleased the Lord to bruise him"(Isaiah 53:10 KJV).

The wrath of God toward us was satisfied when Jesus Christ died on the cross for us. Therefore, we no longer have need to fear His wrath. We have been brought into fellowship with our Father, God, through Jesus Christ.

Is this sacrifice not worth an offering up of our lives to Him?

LOVE MERCY

When Jesus had lifted up himself, and saw none but the woman, he said unto her, "Woman, where are those thine accusers? hath no man condemned thee?" She said, "No man, Lord." And Jesus said unto her, "Neither do I condemn thee: go, and sin no more."

JOHN 8:10-11 KJV

When the load of sin is felt,
And much forgiveness known;
Then the heart of course will melt,
Though hard before as stone:
Blame not then her love and tears,
Greatly she in debt has been;
But I have removed her fears,
And pardoned all her sin.
When I read this woman's case,
Her love and humble zeal;
I confess, with shame of face,
My heart is made of steel.
Much has been forgiv'n to me,
JESUS paid my heavy score;
What a creature must I be
That I can love no more!

-JOHN NEWTON

It is very easy to justify our own sins. Yet, when others sin, it is just as easy to condemn. How great the tears in the heart of God when we judge our neighbor, whom God commands us to love and forgive. The sin in our hearts is multiplied when we do not love mercy. The Bible tells us to "do justly, and to love mercy, and to walk humbly with thy God" (Micah 6:8 KJV).

When we do not love mercy, we condemn the sins of others rather than praying that God would forgive them. But such an attitude of condemnation only multiplies the sin that exists in the heart of the one condemning.

Let us love mercy. Not only because it keeps others from falling under our own condemnation, but also because it keeps us from being condemned by our own words. Yet, when we are forgiving and loving, even to the worst of sinners, we show the compassion and love of Christ, who gave His life for us while we were sinners.

WHAT IS TRUTH?

Jesus saith unto him, "I am the way, the truth, and the life: no man cometh unto the Father, but by me."

JOHN 14:6 KJV

What is truth? Every major religion in the world claims that it is the truth. Yet, our Savior Jesus Christ says that He is "the way, the truth, and the life." Clearly, this puts us in a dilemma, if we dare allow ourselves to be tempted to entertain the questions of our day about the truth of God.

To question the truth is nothing new. In Jesus' day, Pontius Pilate asked the same question, "What is truth?" (John 18:38 KJV)

No answer came from the mouth of Jesus after this monumental question. Beyond any doubt, the truth was standing in front of Pilate's face. His chance had come, and later, his Answer was crucified.

Many in this world question the truth without receiving the truth. So many refuse to realize that truth is not something to be questioned, but something to be embraced. The truth is a Person whom the sting of death could not hold. He laid down His life and rose again from the dead to dwell in the hearts of those who would believe. Those who believe have complete assurance of the Truth. For in Christ, we must believe before we see.

We all have questions about certain things in life and in the Bible. But all of those questions boil down to whether or not we believe the words of Jesus Christ. He called himself the "truth."

What will you do with the Truth today? Will you embrace the Truth, or will you, as Pilate did, cast it away? The next time you are tempted to question the truth, turn your "What" into "Who," and ask yourself, "Who is Truth?" Then, remember the words of our Lord.

UNIFIED IN OUR HUNGER

Righteousness exalteth a nation: but sin is a reproach to any people.

PROVERBS 14:34 KJV

Around the year 1620, a Dutch vessel brought African slaves to the colony of Jamestown, Virginia. These were the first men and women to be brought as slaves to the mainland of what would become the United States of America. The very moment that the ship met the American shore, it changed forever the history of the nation that would rise out of this new world.

Yet, the great nineteenth-century preacher John B. Meachum saw something far deeper than mere history. He saw souls. He saw a nation of people whose redemption relied fully upon their hunger after God and their unity towards one another.

God has formed man out of clay, and all nations have sprung there from. It is therefore not natural for man to hate his fellow, but it is to be traced to other causes. Shall we then who are of the same species, same color, cultivate and cherish a principle so contrary to reason and scripture and in its consequences so direful and disastrous?

Our people can only distinguish themselves as a nation by

"fearing God" and "working righteousness," for "righteousness exalteth a nation, but sin is a reproach to any people." We must therefore be united in love and affection—our interests, aims, and hopes must be one—for in the language of the text, "Behold how good and how pleasant it is for brethren to dwell together in unity!" We must cultivate all the Christian graces which the apostle Peter recommends—"add to your faith virtue, and to virtue knowledge, and to knowledge temperance, and to temperance patience, and to patience godliness, and to godliness brotherly kindness, and to brotherly kindness charity." Upon the exercise of these graces and Christian qualities depend our elevation in this life and our eternal happiness in the world to come.

We must have union—we can and must have it, else we shall remain in darkness, ignorance, and superstition, in a state of moral and intellectual degradation.

-JOHN B. MEACHUM

Times have not changed as greatly as it seems. Today, we must still hunger for the righteousness and holiness of God. The same Jesus who redeemed our ancestors from the shame of slavery is the same Jesus who will propel us into the fullness of His purpose, if we allow it. We can assuredly propel into our purpose here in this "new world," if only we become unified in our hunger for the holiness of God.

You Can Do Nothing

[Jesus said,] "Without me ye can do nothing."

JOHN 15:5 KJV

In everything the life of the branch is to be the exact counterpart of that of the Vine. Of himself Jesus had said: "The Son can do nothing of himself." As the outcome of that entire dependence, He could add: "All that the Father doeth, doeth the Son also likewise." As Son He did not receive His life from the Father once for all, but moment by moment. His life was a continual waiting on the Father for all He was to do. And so Christ says of His disciples: "Ye can do nothing apart from Me." He means it literally. To everyone who wants to live the true disciple life, to bring forth fruit and glorify God, the message comes: You can do nothing. What had been said: "He that abideth in me, and I in him, the same beareth much fruit," is here enforced by the simplest and strongest of arguments: "Abiding in Me is indispensable, for, you know it, of yourselves you can do nothing to maintain or act out the heavenly life."

A deep conviction of the truth of this word lies at the very root of a strong spiritual life. As little as I created myself, as little as I could raise a man from the dead, can I give myself the divine life. As little as I can give it myself, can I maintain or increase it: every motion is the work of God through Christ and His Spirit. It is as a man believes this that he will take up that position of entire and continual dependence, which is the very essence of the life of faith. With the spiritual eye he sees Christ every moment supplying grace for every breathing and every deepening of the spiritual life. His whole heart says Amen to the word: You can do nothing. And just because he does so, he can also say: "I can do all things in Christ who strengtheneth me." The sense of helplessness, and the abiding to which it compels, leads to true fruitfulness and diligence in good works.

Apart from me ye can do nothing. What a plea and what a call every moment to abide in Christ! We have only to go back to the vine to see how true it is. Look again at that little branch, utterly helpless and fruitless except as it receives sap from the vine, and learn that the full conviction of not being able to do anything apart from Christ is just what you need to teach you to abide in your heavenly Vine. It is this that is the great meaning of the pruning Christ spoke of—all that is self must be brought low, that our confidence may be in Christ alone. "Abide in me"—much fruit! "Apart from me"—nothing! Ought there to be any doubt as to what we shall choose?

-ANDREW MURRAY

SHINE!

[Jesus said,] "Ye are the light of the world. A city that is set on an
hill cannot be hid. Neither do men light a candle, and put it under a
bushel, but on a candlestick; and it giveth light unto all that are in
the house. Let your light so shine before men, that they may see your
good works, and glorify your Father which is in heaven."

MATTHEW 5:14-16 KJV

One of the most blessed things about being a Christian is
our ability to shine, no matter how dark this world becomes.
In a world that has increased in ungodliness, isn't it good to
know that we can make a difference? God intended for it to
be that way. He wants our light to shine so that we can glorify
our Heavenly Father.

If the world seems cold to you,
Kindle fires to warm it!
Let their comfort hide from view
Winters that deform it.
Hearts as frozen as your own
To that radiance gather;
You will soon forget to moan,
"Ah, the cheerless weather!"

If the world's a wilderness,
Go build houses in it!

Will it help your loneliness
On the winds to din it?
Raise a hut, however slight;
Weeds and brambles smother;
And to roof and meal invite
Some forlorner brother.

If the world's a vale of tears,
Smile till rainbows span it!
Breathe the love that life endears,
Clear from clouds to fan it.
Of your gladness lend a gleam
Unto souls that shiver;
Show them how dark Sorrow's stream
Blends with Hope's bright river."

-JOANNA P. MOORE

You can shine today. God has enabled you to walk into a world of sorrow and bring joy, peace, and love. And once you begin to see the blessing of shining your light, you will never want to stop.

THE RACE IS NOT OVER

[Jesus said,] "He that endureth to the end shall be saved."

MATTHEW 10:22 KJV

In any marathon, there are those who come in first place, second place, and so forth, but all of those who finish the race are considered winners and true athletes. All of them are worthy of reward. The reason is that they finished the race that was placed before them. Many of those who have gone before us have finished their race. They fought physical and spiritual battles on our behalf. They suffered persecution and hardship, not willing to give up in the middle of their painful struggle. Because they kept running their race on our behalf, we enjoy many of the freedoms and liberties we have today.

God has also called us to run a race. But this race is not one that is won by those who are swift or strong. It is won by those who finish—whether they are swift, strong, weak, or slow. No matter how much or how little you have, God has given you enough to complete this Christian walk to the very end.

To finish our race is vital to future generations. They are in great need of seeing authentic Christians truly love God and each other. And they are watching closer than you may think. They are depending on you to finish your race so that they can start theirs. You have the power to finish. No matter how long the road ahead is, stay your course. Even when it seems that life is out of control, remember the One who is paving the road before you. Nothing in this world is impossible to you if only you believe, and keep on believing in Him. With every step of this marathon of life, the Lord is with you, strengthening and encouraging you. If you look to Him, you will finish this race. And at the finish line, God's reward will be waiting.

-BROTHER ANDREW

LORD, TEACH US TO PRAY

It came to pass, that, as he was praying in a certain place, when he
ceased, one of his disciples said unto him, Lord, teach us to pray.

LUKE 11:1 KJV

Anyone who has ever driven for an extended amount of
time knows that there are many people who drive, giving no
proof at all that they know how to do so. The same is true for
prayer. Most people in this world pray in some form or another. Yet, few really know how to pray. For this reason, Andrew
Murray wrote the following:

"Lord, teach us to pray." Yes, to pray. This is what we need
to be taught. Though in its beginnings prayer is so simple that
the feeblest child can pray, yet it is at the same time the highest and holiest work to which man can rise. It is fellowship
with the Unseen and Most Holy One. The powers of the
eternal world have been placed at its disposal. It is the very
essence of true religion, the channel of all blessings, the secret
of power and life. Not only for ourselves, but for others, for
the Church, for the world, it is to prayer that God has given
the right to take hold of Him and His strength. It is on
prayer that the promises wait for their fulfilment, the kingdom for its coming, the glory of God for its full revelation.

And for this blessed work, how slothful and unfit we are. It is only the Spirit of God can enable us to do it aright.

-ANDREW MURRAY

One can only pray by allowing God to pray through him or her. This "praying through" demands a submission and reverence that places our innermost being in tune with God's Spirit. If you belong to Christ, you have the resources within you to submit in such a way.

Once you have truly begun to pray, there is nothing in this world that is out of your reach, which the Father desires you to have. In your own prayer closet, you can be a blessing to others, yourself, and to God himself as you lift your prayers of worship to Him. Why not let today become a day of commitment to seek the face of God?

ONLY BELIEVING

Faith is the substance of things hoped for, the evidence of things not seen.

HEBREWS 11:1 KJV

What is faith? For many of us, the asking of this question brings certain words to mind such as trust, reliance, or even confidence. Others of us immediately quote Hebrews 11:1 to define the word. Yet, do our experiences in life line up with those meanings? In *The Christian's Secret of a Happy Life*, Hannah Whitall Smith explains faith in a life-changing way:

Your idea of faith, I suppose, has been something like this. You have looked upon it as in some way a sort of thing, either a religious exercise of soul or an inward gracious disposition of heart. You have thought of it as something tangible that when you have obtained it, you can look at and rejoice over and use as a passport to God's favor or a coin with which to purchase His gifts. And you have been praying for faith, expecting all the while to get something like this and never having received any such thing, you are insisting upon it that you have no faith.

Now faith, in fact, is not in the least this sort of thing. It is nothing at all tangible. It is simply believing God, and, like sight, it is nothing apart from its object. You might as well shut your eyes and look inside to see whether you have sight as to look inside to discover whether you have faith. You see something, and thus know that you have sight; you believe something, and thus know that you have faith. For, as sight is only seeing, so faith is only believing.

-HANNAH WHITALL SMITH

Faith is only believing. And to believe is to trust that something is true. If we are to embrace God's Word as truth, we will have all of the faith we will ever need, and nothing will be impossible to us.

HE WILL BRING THE ANSWER

This is the confidence that we have in him, that, if we ask any thing according to his will, he heareth us: And if we know that he hear us, whatsoever we ask, we know that we have the petitions that we desired of him.

1 JOHN 5:14-15 KJV

We have a great promise in Scripture of God's involvement in our lives when we pray. In our prayer closet, the greatest Power in the universe stands by, ready to answer us according to His perfect will. Who can stand against such authority as the will of God? No one. Yet, it is our simple prayers that stir the heart of the God of all creation. Do we dare to ever overlook such an incredible opportunity?

If prayer puts God to work on earth, then, by the same token, prayerlessness rules God out of the world's affairs and prevents Him from working. And if prayer moves God to work in this world's affairs, then prayerlessness excludes God from everything concerning men and leaves man on earth the mere creature of circumstances, at the mercy of blind fate or without help of any kind from God. It leaves man in this world with its tremendous responsibilities and its difficult problems and with all of its sorrows, burdens, and afflictions, without any God at all. In reality the denial of prayer is a denial of God himself, for God and prayer are so inseparable that they can never be divorced.

-E. M. BOUNDS

All who claim to know God must be people of prayer. We must be people who are eager to fellowship with the one who has rescued us from a world that has purposed itself to slow us down. But our progress need not be decelerated. We can move forward into our destiny and purpose without even having to slow down. The God who listens and answers is there for us at all times, when we approach His throne in all humility, when we call upon Him. Then, He will open up our eyes and show us things that we could have never known ourselves. He will bring the answer, if only we will pray.

Prayer: A Matter of Life

[The Lord said,] If my people, which are called by my name, shall humble themselves, and pray, and seek my face, and turn from their wicked ways; then will I hear from heaven, and will forgive their sin, and will heal their land.

2 Chronicles 7:14 KJV

We can truly love God with our entire lives as we offer ourselves when we pray. But what really do we seek when we approach God's glorious throne? Do we really seek what is truly good? Or, do we, as many, seek those things that benefit only ourselves?

Consider this classic writing:

O! How few there are who pray! For how few are they who desire what is truly good! Crosses, external and internal humiliation, renouncement of our own wills, the death of self and the establishment of God's throne upon the ruins of self love, these are indeed good. Not to desire these is not to pray; to desire them seriously, soberly, constantly, and with reference to all the details of life, this is true prayer. Not to desire them and yet to suppose we pray is an illusion like that of the wretched who dream themselves happy. Alas! How many souls full of self and of an imaginary desire for perfection in the midst of hosts of voluntary imperfections, have never yet uttered this true prayer of the heart! It is in reference to this that St. Augustine says: "He that loveth little, prayeth little; he that loveth much, prayeth much."

-FENELON AND MADAME JEANNE GUYON

Let us all condition our hearts when we pray, so that we can approach God's presence in a way that pleases Him. Then, His Word assures us that "he is a rewarder of them that diligently seek him" (Hebrews 11:6 KJV) and no good thing will He withhold from us.

THE STRANGER

[Jesus said,] "I was an hungered, and ye gave me meat: I was thirsty, and ye gave me drink: I was a stranger, and ye took me in: Naked, and ye clothed me: I was sick, and ye visited me: I was in prison, and ye came unto me."

MATTHEW 25:35-36 KJV

We all enjoy receiving promotion and credit for a job well done. But should those things be the reason why we live and work? It can often be tempting to demand recognition for the things we do well. But if we take our eyes off God, the One who enabled us to do those things, it can put us in a place where we can lose all that we have. As you will see in the story below by Sundar Singh, it does not matter who gets the credit, as long as God gets the glory.

Once on a dark night I went alone into the forest to pray, and seating myself upon a rock I lay before God my deep necessities and besought His help. After a short time, seeing a poor man coming towards me, I thought he had come to ask me for some relief because he was hungry and cold. I said to him, "I am a poor man, and except this blanket I have nothing at all. You had better go to the village near by and ask for help there." And lo! Even whilst I was saying this he flashed forth like lightning, and, showering drops of blessing, immediately disappeared. Alas! Alas! It was now clear to me that this was my beloved Master who came not to beg from a poor creature like me, but to bless and to enrich me (2 Corinthians 8:9), and so I was left weeping and lamenting my folly and lack of insight.

On another day, my work being finished, I again went into the forest to pray, and seated upon that same rock began to consider for what blessings I should make petition. Whilst thus engaged it seemed to me that another came and stood near me, who, judged by his bearing and dress and manner of speech, appeared to be a revered and devoted servant of God; but his eyes glittered with craft and cunning, and as he spoke he seemed to breathe an odour of hell.

He thus addressed me, "Holy and Honoured Sir, pardon me for interrupting your prayers and breaking in on your privacy; but it is one's duty to seek to promote the advantage of others, and therefore I have come to lay an important matter before you. Your pure and unselfish life has made a deep impression not only on me, but upon a great number of devout persons. But although in the Name of God you have sacrificed yourself body and soul for others, you have never been truly appreciated. My meaning is that being a Christian only a few thousand Christians have come under your influence, and some even of these distrust you. How much better would it be if you became a Hindu or a Muslim, and thus become a great leader indeed? They are in search of such a spiritual head. If you accept this suggestion of mine, then three hundred and ten millions of Hindus and Muslims will become your followers and render you reverent homage."

As soon as I heard this there rushed from my lips these words, "Thou Satan! Get thee hence. I knew at once that thou wert a wolf in sheep's clothing! Thy one wish is that I should give up the Cross and the narrow path that leads to life, and choose the broad road of death. My Master himself is my lot and my portion, who himself gave His life for me, and it behooves me to offer as a sacrifice my life and all I have to Him who is all in all to me. Get you gone therefore, for with you I have nothing to do."

Hearing this he went off grumbling and growling in his rage. And I, in tears, thus poured out my soul to God in prayer, "My Lord God, my all in all, life of my life, and spirit of my spirit, look in mercy upon me and so fill me with Thy Holy Spirit that my heart shall have no room for love of aught but Thee."

-SUNDAR SINGH

WHAT IS GOOD?

He hath shewed thee, O man, what is good; and what doth the Lord require of thee, but to do justly, and to love mercy, and to walk humbly with thy God?

MICAH 6:8 KJV

We can become the most learned people in the world; perhaps even the wealthiest people to ever walk this earth. We can accomplish great things in science, art, athletics, and politics. We can raise the most beautiful children into the most productive adults. Yet in God's eyes, this is not what is good. We can develop medicines to cure diseases. We can even feed the mouths of the poor so that no one in the world has to go to bed hungry. We can establish enough churches to fill cities across the country. Yet, without doing justly, loving mercy, and walking humbly, we have done no good at all.

What good does it do to speak learnedly about the Trinity if, lacking humility, you displease the Trinity? Indeed it is not learning that makes a man holy and just, but a virtuous life makes him pleasing to God. I would rather feel contrition than know how to define it. For what would it profit us to know the whole Bible by heart and the principles of all the philosophers if we live without grace and the love of God?

Vanity of vanities and all is vanity, except to love God and serve Him alone.

-THOMAS À KEMPIS

How great it would be, if we would give our lives to loving God and serving Him alone. As African Americans, we have accomplished many things. But one thing is needful, and one thing we must never stray away from is this: to pursue and follow after the heart of our Father, God, without reserve. Without Him, we have only limited potential as a people. Without a humble spirit, we cannot approach His throne to accomplish very much. Can we commit ourselves to loving Him and serving Him alone? Can we do justly, love mercy, and walk humbly before Him? If so, then we can walk in His favor and accomplish more than we could ever imagine.

BLACK IS BEAUTIFUL

Dark am I, yet lovely, O daughters of Jerusalem, dark like the tents of Kedar, like the tent curtains of Solomon.

SONG OF SOLOMON 1:5 NIV

All of God's people are glorious in beauty, and that includes you. Very seldom is darkness associated with beauty, but the beloved of King Solomon was, in his eyes, perfect in beauty. So are you, in God's eyes.

Solomon's father, David, recognized this: "I praise you because I am fearfully and wonderfully made; your works are wonderful, I know that full well" (Psalm 139:14 NIV).

Do you know fully well that you are beautiful? Do you know that you are a wonderful part of God's creation? Well, you are. So beautiful, in fact, that such splendor is worthy of the praises of God. Yes, you can praise God because you are the apple of His eye—gloriously created, fearfully and wonderfully made.

Today, when you look at the person in the mirror, don't focus on what needs to change. Don't concern yourself with how much weight you need to lose or gain. Don't concern yourself with what needs to happen with your hair, your scars, or your skin. Look into your eyes, and gaze upon the person God made. When God formed you in your mother's womb, knowing how you would look when you became older, it was perfect. In fact, He said, "Behold, I have graven thee upon the palms of my hands" (Isaiah 49:16 KJV). What you see in the mirror is exactly what He wanted. Be glad about it, because your appearance brought enough joy to the heart of God for Him to create you just the way you are. You are black, and you are beautiful.

THE CURSE OF NORMALCY

Ye are a chosen generation, a royal priesthood, an holy nation, a peculiar people; that ye should shew forth the praises of him who hath called you out of darkness into his marvellous light.

1 PETER 2:9 KJV

When many of us were children, all we wanted to do was "fit in," to blend in with the norms of our surroundings so we would be better liked and appreciated. Some still yearn for this today. While these desires are understandable, God wants us to "fit in" with Him, rather than the normalcy of this world. Martin Luther King understood this in his passion for equality. His message still resonates just as strongly today as it did years ago:

There was a time when the church was very powerful in the time when the early Christians rejoiced at being deemed worthy to suffer for what they believed. In those days the church was not merely a thermometer that recorded the ideas and principles of popular opinion; it was a thermostat that transformed the mores of society. Whenever the early Christians entered a town, the people in power became disturbed and immediately sought to convict the Christians for being "disturbers of the peace" and "outside agitators." But the

Christians pressed on, in the conviction that they were "a colony of heaven," called to obey God rather than man. Small in number, they were big in commitment. They were too God-intoxicated to be "astronomically intimidated." By their effort and example they brought an end to such ancient evils as infanticide and gladiatorial contests.

Things are different now. So often the contemporary church is a weak, ineffectual voice with an uncertain sound. So often it is an arch-defender of the status quo. Far from being disturbed by the presence of the church, the power structure of the average community is consoled by the church's silent and often even vocal sanction of things as they are.

But the judgment of God is upon the church as never before. If today's church does not recapture the sacrificial spirit of the early church, it will lose its authenticity, forfeit the loyalty of millions, and be dismissed as an irrelevant social club with no meaning for the twentieth century.

-MARTIN LUTHER KING JR.

VICTORY OVER PRESSURE

The trial of your faith, being much more precious than of gold that perisheth, though it be tried with fire, might be found unto praise and honour and glory at the appearing of Jesus Christ.

1 PETER 1:7 KJV

What should we do with the circumstances of our lives? Do we accept them? Do we bemoan them? Or, do we change them? God has given us everything we need in order to not just endure, but to triumph over our circumstances so that we can bring honor and glory to God. Booker T. Washington (1856-1915) was one of those who chose to triumph over his limitations and bring honor to God.

It has been my fortune to be associated all my life with a problem—a hard, perplexing, but important problem. There was a time when I looked upon this fact as a great misfortune. It seemed to me a great hardship that I was born poor, and it seemed to me a greater hardship that I should have been born a Negro. I did not like to admit, even to myself, that I felt this way about the matter., because, it seemed to me an indication of weakness and cowardice for any man to complain about the condition he was born to.

Later, I came to the conclusion that it was not only weak

and cowardly, but that it was a mistake to think of the matter in the way in which I had done. I came to see that, along with his disadvantages, the Negro in America had some advantages, and I made up my mind that opportunities that had been denied him from without could be more than made up by greater concentration and power within.

Perhaps I can illustrate what I mean by a fact I learned while I was in school. I recall my teacher's explaining to the class one day how it was that steam or any other form of energy, if allowed to escape and dissipate itself, loses its value as a motive power. Energy must be confined; steam must be locked in a boiler in order to generate power.

The same thing seems to have been true in the case of the Negro. Where the Negro has met with discrimination and with difficulties because of his race, he has invariably tended to get up more steam. When this steam has been rightly directed and controlled, it has become a great force in the up-building of the race. If, on the contrary, it merely spent itself on fruitless agitation and hot air, no good has come of it.

-BOOKER T. WASHINGTON

EVANGELIZER OF THE WORLD

*Wherefore I put thee in remembrance
that thou stir up the gift of God.*

2 TIMOTHY 1:6 KJV

Have you ever wondered if there was a greater purpose to slavery? Were our ancestors shackled and subjected to unthinkable cruelty just for the devil's sake, or was there a greater purpose that went beyond the adversaries schemes? Over a century ago, Matthew Anderson had an idea about such a purpose that we should take heed to today:

I have long believed, that in some way, I know not how, and at some time, I know not when, the Negro is going to become a mighty power for good, under God, in this country. For I do not believe God designed that that brawny arm, cheerful life, fertile brain, and productive power of the Negro were to be employed for no other purpose than the hewing of wood and drawing of water. God is too wise to imply His instruments in this way. The mind that has within it powers which when drawn out and developed will be able to weigh the stars, map out the heavens, and read the destinies, was not designed to forever be a digger of a ditch or a fawner at a table. The trials through which the Negro is now passing; the prejudice, the slanders, the misrepresentation, the injustice, and the hardships are employed simply as correctives to fit him for this great future.

But in saying this, I do not mean to imply that the Negro is designed to supplant the white man, or any other man. He has not been, nor never will be, a supplanter. His mission shall be, as it ever has been, that of a teacher of the great fundamental truths of the Bible, namely, the Fatherhood of God and the brotherhood of men, Christ Jesus the hope of the world, and the right of all men to life, liberty, and the pursuit of happiness. These truths the Negro is teaching now by his remarkable patience, perseverance, endurance, and faith, though by few recognized and acknowledged. Then, it will be acknowledged by all and he will assume his place as the great teacher and evangelizer of the world.

-MATTHEW ANDERSON

Has God commissioned the black race to such a great responsibility? As this nation becomes increasingly godless, could the key to great revival be in the hands of we, who came here as slaves? With God, this is clearly possible, but is it possible with you? Can you take a stand and let Christ shine through you wherever you go?

Let us not allow the blood of our fathers and mothers to be in vain. Unbeknownest to many of them, they came here for Jesus. Let us commit ourselves daily to fulfilling that calling.

LAYING A FOUNDATION

Then answered I them, and said unto them, The God of heaven, he will prosper us; therefore we his servants will arise and build: but ye have no portion, nor right, nor memorial, in Jerusalem.

NEHEMIAH 2:20 KJV

Our forefathers were handed a very difficult life to endure. But still, they overcame. It could be that they overcame because they were simply trying to survive and endure their hardship. But even so, their survival and endurance is exactly what we needed. They worked jobs considered menial. They were discriminated against. They avoided certain cities and neighborhoods for safety's sake. They often fought the temptation to avenge, just for our sake. They never gave up. Today, their toil and labor has brought our generation to a much better place.

In a great sermon, which I once heard Phillips Brooks preach, he used a sentence something like this:"One generation gathers the material and the next generation builds the palaces." He simply meant by that, that one generation laid the foundation for the succeeding generation. The earlier generation is always the one which has to deal very largely with the rougher affairs of life, in order that the next generation might have the privilege of dealing with the higher and finer affairs of life.

I repeat that sentence for the sake of emphasis, for I want you to think about it; "One generation gathers the material and the other builds the palaces." Now this is true of all generations; all people; that one generation has got to lay the foundation for the next generation, and unless the foundation is properly laid—is deeply laid—it is impossible for the succeeding generation to have a very successful career.

-BOOKER T. WASHINGTON

Clearly, our generation has much more to do. But today, we are building palaces and gathering the material for much greater things for the next generation. And the God of Heaven is working alongside us, helping us through it all. It is He who will cause the black race in America to rise up and prosper, as we remember the sacrifices that were made before us.

SAVED FROM DESPAIR

*[Jesus] is able also to save them to the uttermost that come unto God
by him, seeing he ever liveth to make intercession for them.*

HEBREWS 7:25 KJV

God saved us to the uttermost. This means that there is
nothing more to do. The work is done, completely. Aren't you
glad He has done a complete work for the sake of your soul?
Today, we can draw near, never to fear His rejection as we call
upon Him. What an honor it is to be a Christian!

> *My former hopes are dead,*
> *My terror now begins;*
> *I feel, alas! that I am dead*
> *In trespasses and sins.*
> *Ah, whither shall I fly?*
> *I hear the thunder roar*
> *The law proclaims destruction nigh,*
> *And vengeance at the door.*
> *When I review my ways,*
> *I dread impending doom;*
> *But sure, a friendly whisper says,*
> *"Flee from the wrath to come."*
> *I see, or think I see,*

A glimm'ring from afar;
A beam of day that shines for me,
To save me from despair.
Fore-runner of the sun,
It marks the Pilgrim's way;
I'll gaze upon it while I run,
And watch the rising day.

-JOHN NEWTON

Life certainly gets brighter when we look forward to all the glimmer of the brightening day, the shining brightness and light of God that awaits us ahead. It comes to shine upon us steadily and surely. It is not according to our works, but His grace. If it depended on our works, we would have to earn our way into His presence. But He simply asks that we call upon Him. Once we have called upon Him, He is there, and there is nothing that will draw Him away except our own doubts and fears.

Won't you call on Him today? Will you beseech Him even for a moment to save you from the trials and despair of this world? Will you call Him for an assurance of security in this ever-changing society? He is waiting for you to "Flee from the wrath to come." He is waiting to give you the strength and power to endure in His strength. Will you go to Him?

THE HAPPY MIND

Humble yourselves therefore under the mighty hand of God, that he may exalt you in due time: Casting all your care upon him; for he careth for you.

1 PETER 5:6-7 KJV

He cares for you. Perhaps the greatest of all Bible promises starts here. With this awesome statement in mind, there is nothing in the world that should be able to make us downcast and depressed. Now, it is up to us to walk in such a promise and be glad that God, who is infinite in understanding, will truly show that He cares for us.

Out upon the haughty calf, I say
Who turns his grumbling head away,
And quarrels with his feed of hay
Because it is not clover.

Give to me the happy mind
That will ever seek and ever find,
Something good and something kind
All this wide world over.

"Don't look for the faults as you go through life,

And even when you find them
It is wise and kind, to be somewhat blind,
And look for the virtues behind them.

"Never look sad, there's nothing so bad
As getting familiar with sorrow;
Treat him to-day in a chivalrous way,
And he will seek other quarters to-morrow.

"Let each day carry away
Its own little burden of sorrow,
Or you may miss one-half of the bliss
That comes in the lap of to-morrow."

-JOANNA P. MOORE

PRAYER: THE CHRISTIAN'S WEAPON OF WAR

We wrestle not against flesh and blood, but against principalities,
against powers, against the rulers of the darkness of this world,
against spiritual wickedness in high places.

EPHESIANS 6:12 KJV

What various hindrances we meet
In coming to a mercy-seat?
Yet who that knows the worth of prayer,
But wishes to be often there.
Prayer makes the darkened cloud withdraw,
Prayer climbs the ladder Jacob saw;
Gives exercise to faith and love,
Brings every blessing from above.
Restraining prayer, we cease to fight;
Prayer makes the Christian's armor bright;
And Satan trembles, when he sees
The weakest saint upon his knees.

-JOHN NEWTON

Did you know that of all the talk about the Devil, you are more powerful on your worst day than he is on his best day?

We do indeed wrestle with principalities and powers, but we do not do so from a weak position. For, although we must confront spiritual wickedness in high places, the Bible says that we are "seated with Him in heavenly places." This means that although the adversary is in high places, we are in higher places. We are seated with Christ, who is far more powerful than anything that comes our way.

If ever you face a challenge that is too large, and too over-whelming to handle, remember that God is greater than even the most powerful challenges. Remember that His presence lives within you. He longs to touch through you the affairs of your life. All you have to do is trust in His Word. But it is this reading of the Word that is so often hindered.

We face more hindrances to prayer and Bible reading than perhaps any other thing in our lives. Have you ever wondered why? It is because our adversary, the Devil, knows that if you ever truly receive a fresh revelation from God and a life-changing touch from Heaven, you will triumph over him at every turn. Looking at the details of your life, perhaps you might conclude that more prayer and more revelation of God's Word are needed. There is no reason to wait another day.

WHAT A FRIEND!

If a man say, I love God, and hateth his brother, he is a liar:
for he that loveth not his brother whom he hath seen,
how can he love God whom he hath not seen?

1 JOHN 4:20 KJV

The love that God showed us through Jesus' death on the cross could not have been greater. When we were lost in our sins, He took the penalty of our shameful deeds and died so that we could live. But the greatest news of all is that this Friend who died for us is alive today, so that we can live for Him. But have you ever wondered how to really live for Jesus?

Living for Jesus is all about loving Him and loving your neighbor. This great commandment embraces every other commandment in the Bible. When we live according to it, we extend an arm of friendship toward God, who in turn reaches out to us. And even though we often fall short, Jesus loves us in spite of our failings. He embraces us when we are more consumed with our own lives than our relationship with Christ. He still loves us, even when we fail to express our love for Him. He accepts us and forgives our sins.

Look around you. Is there anyone who you feel does not deserve your respect or your love? Has your life been ravaged by one bad relationship after another? Remember, God forgave and loved you. And because of this, you are free to love your neighbor with the grace and love of Jesus.

FOR HIS GLORY

*"Whatsoever ye shall ask in my name,
that will I do, that the Father
may be glorified in the Son."*

JOHN 14:13 KJV

All of us have faced times in life when we needed something from God. Usually, these are the times when we start to pray. Have you ever prayed for something but felt that you did not receive an answer to that prayer? Very often in our Christian life, we will experience times when our wants and needs don't appear to be met. Questions abound as to why the answers never came.

God never promised that we would live a life without problems. Neither did He promise that we could write our own ticket with Him. Stated plainly, He will not give us everything we want. But there is a bright side to all of this. He will give us anything we need in order to bring glory to Him.

Does your desire bring glory to God? If so, you have a limitless promise of provision. You have the privilege of living life under an open Heaven, and the problems you face are temporary. God will not withhold anything from the person who desires to use what they get to bring glory to God. He will equip you and furnish you with the resources of Heaven, that the Father may be glorified in the Son. All you have to do is ask.

INTEGRITY

For ever, O Lord, thy word is settled in heaven. Thy faithfulness is unto all generations: thou hast established the earth, and it abideth.

PSALM 119:89-90

Booker T. Washington once said, "Character is power." Such a statement is a far cry from our modern saying, "Money is power." Yet, the truth of Mr. Washington's statement rings clear.

One of the most challenged areas of Christian life is the issue of integrity. The lack of such a character trait drags the Christian into a life of double standards, moral uncertainty, and a lack of trustworthiness. But what does it mean to have character?

Character is when you are not just willing, but settled on doing exactly what you said you would do. This affects every area of our lives and empowers us in ways that can change our lives and the lives of others.

What impact do you suppose it would cause if God did not have integrity? What would have happened if Jesus, struggling to carry His cross up Golgotha's hill, had decided to throw His cross to the ground and discontinue His redemptive work? What would happen if God suddenly decided that He would not save or heal or provide? For anyone who depends on Him, the impact would be devastating.

In this world, there are expectations for those who call themselves followers of Christ. Our integrity is being watched. Are we faithful to the command to be holy? Are we loving as we should be? Are we trusting God? The answers to these questions will determine our level of integrity in the eyes of the world.

Let us settle within us that we will keep God's Word hidden in our hearts so that the integrity of our Christian witness will be secure.

'TWAS FAITH ALONE THAT SUSTAINED ME

I am crucified with Christ: nevertheless I live; yet not I, but Christ
liveth in me: and the life which I now live in the flesh I live by the
faith of the Son of God, who loved me, and gave himself for me.

GALATIANS 2:20 KJV

In life, we often face challenges that may tempt us to turn
away from God. But these are the difficult times, when we
must turn, more than ever, to God. Martha Griffith Browne
(?-1906) was a female slave, who in the midst of a terrible
beating from her slave-owner, had a vision of glory that sustained her through the most humiliating times of her life.

Surely, 'twas faith alone that sustained me. The present
scene faded away from my vision, and, in fancy, I stood in the
lonely garden of Gethsemane. I saw the darkness and gloom
that overshadowed the earth, when, deserted by His disciples,
our blessed Lord prayed alone. I heard the sighs and groans
that burst from His tortured breast. I saw the bloody sweat,
as prostrate on the earth He lay in the tribulation of mortal
agony.

I saw the inhuman captors, headed by one of His chosen
twelve, come to seize His sacred person. I saw His face uplift-

ed to the mournful heavens, as He prayed to His Father to remove the cup of sorrow. I saw Him bound and led away to death, without a friend to solace Him. Through the various stages of His awful passion, even to the Mount of Crucifixion, to the bloody and sacred Calvary, I followed my Master. I saw Him nailed to the cross, spit upon, vilified and abused, with the thorny crown pressed upon His brow. I heard the rabble shout.

Then I saw the solemn mystery of nature, that did attestation to the awful fact that a fiendish work had been done and the prophecy fulfilled. The veil of the great temple was rent, the sun overcast, and the moon turned to blood; and in my ecstasy of passion, I could have shouted, "Great is Jesus of Nazareth!" Then I beheld Him triumphing over the powers of darkness and death, when, robed in the white garments of the grave, He broke through the rocky sepulchre, and stood before the affrighted guards. His work was done, the propitiation had been made, and he went to His Father.

This same Jesus, whom the civilized world now worship as their Lord, was once lowly, outcast, and despised; born of the most hated people of the world, [He was] despised alike by Jew and Gentile; laid in the manger of a stable at Bethlehem, with no earthly possessions, having not whereon to lay His weary head; buffeted, spit upon; condemned by the high priests and the doctors of law; branded as an impostor, and put to an ignominious death, with every demonstration of public contempt; crucified between two thieves.

This Jesus is worshipped now by those who wear purple

and fine linen. The class which once scorned Him, now offer at His shrine frankincense and myrrh; but, in their adoration of the despised Nazarene, they never remember that He has declared, not once, but many times, that the poor and the lowly are His people. "Forasmuch as you did it unto one of these you did it unto me."

Then let the African trust and hope on—let him still weep and pray in Gethsemane, for a cloud hangs round about him, and when he prays for the removal of this cup of bondage, let him remember to ask, as his blessed Master did, "Thy will, oh Father, and not our own, be done"; still trust in Him who calmed the raging tempest; trust in Jesus of Nazareth! Look beyond the cross, to Christ.

-MARTHA GRIFFITH BROWNE

Let this story serve as a precedent of faith for your current situation. This great woman, who history does not shine upon or celebrate, brought glory to God that day. Never should we say that our trial is too great for God to handle, whether it is enslavement to poverty, sickness, or sin. This woman of faith is our example, for she knew that at that moment, her trial was not too great for God to handle.

Whatever trial you are facing today, let God handle it and let your faith sustain you. Victory is sure to come.

A GREAT WORK

Commit thy way unto the Lord;
trust also in him; and he shall bring it to pass.

PSALM 37:5 KJV

We are all called to do great things in the name of our
Lord Jesus Christ. But many times, it can be hard to see anything inside of us that can produce anything great. At the
moment of his conversion, Frederick Douglass (1818-1895)
faced the same issue. And though his answer came from an
unlikely source, the proof of its timeliness was manifested in
his life from that day forward:

The good old man had told me, that the "Lord had a great
work for me to do"; and I must prepare to do it; and that he
had been shown that I must preach the Gospel. His words
made a deep impression on my mind, and I verily felt that
some such work was before me, though I could not see how I
should ever engage in its performance. "The good Lord," he
said, "would bring it to pass in his own good time," and that I
must go on reading and studying the scriptures.

The advice and the suggestions of Uncle Lawson, were not
without their influence upon my character and destiny. He
threw my thoughts into a channel from which they have never

entirely diverged. He fanned my already intense love of knowledge into a flame, by assuring me that I was to be a useful man in the world. When I would say to him, "How can these things be—and what can I do?" his simple reply was, "Trust in the Lord." When I told him that "I was a slave, and a slave FOR LIFE," he said, "the Lord can make you free, my dear. All things are possible with him, only have faith in God." "Ask, and it shall be given." "If you want liberty," said the good old man, "ask the Lord for it, in faith, AND HE WILL GIVE IT TO YOU."

Thus assured, and cheered on, under the inspiration of hope, I worked and prayed with a light heart, believing that my life was under the guidance of a wisdom higher than my own. With all other blessings sought at the mercy seat, I always prayed that God would, of His great mercy, and in His own good time, deliver me from my bondage.

-FREDERICK DOUGLASS

God delivered Mr. Douglass from his bondage. His bondage was the evil of slavery. What bondage do you suppose is holding you back from all that God has called you to? Can you trust Him and ask Him in faith to deliver you today?

JEWEL OF GREAT PRICE

Yea doubtless, and I count all things but loss for the excellency of the knowledge of Christ Jesus my Lord: for whom I have suffered the loss of all things, and do count them but dung, that I may win Christ.

PHILIPPIANS 3:8 KJV

What would you do with a jewel of great price? What would you do if such a jewel were worth more than all the substance you have ever seen in your life? If you had to lose everything in order to attain such a jewel, would you do it? Most of us would, knowing that if we had this precious jewel we could, with it, get back everything we had lost.

God is our jewel of great price. Knowing Him is worth giving up everything because having Him will cause us to attain more than we have ever had.

Make me to part with all the enjoyments of life; nay, even life itself, rather than forfeit this jewel of great price. Blessed are the sufferings that are endured, happy is the death that is undergone for heavenly and immortal truth! I believe that You have prepared for those that love You, everlasting mansions of glory; if I believe You, O eternal happiness; Why does any thing appear difficult that leads to You? Why should I not willingly resist unto blood to obtain You? Why do the vain and empty employments of life take such fast hold of us? O perishing time! Why do You thus bewitch and deceive me? O blessed eternity! When will You be my portion for ever?

-RICHARD ALLEN

What can surpass the joy of knowing God? Is it possible to name one thing? What price can we place on such bliss? Yet, how often do we neglect the very thing we long for? How often do we simply ignore the very thing we need?

Today, this can change. We not only have a desire to see God, but He has a desire to see us. He has made a way for us, through our Lord Jesus Christ. We can enter His presence at any time, in the name of Jesus. Yes, this is the way we enter into the presence of the Father—through Jesus. Will you today? Will you enter into the joy of your desire?

A FENCE OF TRUST

Trust in the Lord with all thine heart; and lean not unto thine own understanding. In all thy ways acknowledge him, and he shall direct thy paths.

PROVERBS 3:5-6 KJV

In this life, we all need something that is higher than ourselves, that can protect us in ways that go beyond our ability to handle. Sometimes our own knowledge and understanding can do little to solve the things we face in life. This is when we have to lay them aside and build around us a "fence of trust."

> *I've built a firm, strong fence of trust,*
> *All around to-day;*
> *I fill the space with loving work*
> *And within it stay.*
> *I look not through the sheltering bars,*
> *Anxious for tomorrow*
> *God does help whatever comes,*
> *Be it joy or sorrow.*

-JOANNA P. MOORE

This fence of trust will surround us with the protection and provision of God, which will repel every evil thing that comes our way. Why not build this fence around your life today?

THE HEART THAT
FOREVER SINGS

What time I am afraid, I will trust in thee. In God I will praise his word, in God I have put my trust; I will not fear what flesh can do unto me.

We have all faced times when life can become so overwhelming that we cannot figure out how to respond. These are the times when we have to simply let go and praise God. Yes, even if it seems as though doing so would be senseless, there truly is power in praise.

True praise that comes from the heart affirms your trust in God. It declares to you, the world, and the adversary that God is in control of everything in your life, whether things seem good or bad.

> *The heart that trusts forever sings,*
> *And feels as light as if it had wings,*
> *A well of joy within it springs,*
> *Come, good or ill, it is God's will.*

-JOANNA P. MOORE

I WILL BE THEIR GOD

[The Lord saith,] I will . . . be their God.

JEREMIAH 31:33 KJV

Christian! Here is all thou canst require. To make thee happy thou wantest something that shall satisfy thee; and is not this enough? If thou canst pour this promise into thy cup, wilt thou not say, with David, "My cup runneth over; I have more than heart can wish"? When this is fulfilled, "I am thy God," art thou not possessor of all things?

Desire is insatiable as death, but He who filleth all in all can fill it. The capacity of our wishes who can measure? But the immeasurable wealth of God can more than overflow it. I ask thee if thou art not complete when God is thine? Dost thou want anything but God? Is not His all-sufficiency enough to satisfy thee if all else should fail? But thou wantest more than quiet satisfaction; thou desirest rapturous delight. Come, soul, here is music fit for Heaven in this thy portion, for God is the Maker of Heaven.

Not all the music blown from sweet instruments, or drawn from living strings, can yield such melody as this sweet promise, "I will be their God." Here is a deep sea of bliss, a shoreless ocean of delight; come, bathe thy spirit in it; swim an age, and thou shalt find no shore; dive throughout eternity, and thou shalt find no bottom. "I will be their God." If this does not make thine eyes sparkle, and thy heart beat high with bliss, then assuredly thy soul is not in a healthy state. But thou wantest more than present delights—thou cravest something concerning which thou mayest exercise hope; and what more canst thou hope for than the fulfillment of this great promise, "I will be their God"?

This is the masterpiece of all the promises; its enjoyment makes a heaven below, and will make a heaven above. Dwell in the light of thy Lord, and let thy soul be always ravished with His love. Get out the marrow and fatness which this portion yields thee. Live up to thy privileges, and rejoice with unspeakable joy.

-CHARLES HADDON SPURGEON

GLORY TO GLORY

*We all, with open face beholding as in a glass the glory of the Lord,
are changed into the same image from glory to glory, even as by the
Spirit of the Lord.*

2 CORINTHIANS 3:18 KJV

What do you see when you look into a mirror? Do you see the glory of the Lord? This is how the Christian looks when you consider the spirit of a person. As we grow spiritually, we are changed and over time appear more and more as the glory of Christ. What greater position or appearance can there be? In what better state can a man or woman ever be? We may not appear as very much to our friends, families, or neighbors, but in the eyes of God, we are beautiful.

When we consider this, how can we ever lose confidence? How can we doubt, when the very object of our faith has created us to appear just as He? The great C. S. Lewis once said: "I believe in Christianity as I believe that the Sun has risen, not only because I see it, but because by it I see everything else." Do others see Him when they look at you?

Knowing who you are, you can rest assured that by the glory that is within you, you can see everything in life. From this shining perspective, you can approach even the greatest of mountains and fearful of devils and never have to draw back.

You look like God. You are made in His image. All else in life pales in comparison to who you are in Him.

Does darkness try to overshadow you? Shine, fellow believer! Let the glory of God within you begin to shine upon the lesser things in life. Show this present world that the God who created everything lives inside your heart!

COMPASSION

Jesus went forth, and saw a great multitude, and was moved with compassion toward them, and he healed their sick.

MATTHEW 14:14 KJV

Have you ever seen a person in such great need that you could no longer keep silent? If so, you can probably acknowledge that the words you spoke and the actions you accomplished represented the absolute best of you. Humankind is at its best when we respond to the compassion that God puts in our hearts.

This compassion is what moved the abolitionists of centuries past. This compassion was so great that it caused blacks and whites to work hand in hand in order to bring freedom to generations. It caused willing people to lay down their lives when they could have remained silent. To the great souls who fought for freedom, compassion was something that caused them to step out of their hiding places and make a difference in this world. It caused them to lay aside their careers, their interests, and even their friends. Responding to compassion became the meaning of their lives.

In the Bible, Jesus was often moved with compassion. This compassion was not just a feeling of empathy for someone in need. It was a living charge to do something about what was wrong. Is there a circumstance that you see in the life of another that demands action? Are you moved with compassion towards a person, a group, or a cause? If so, your response may bring out the very best of you—that person who can make a difference.

THE POWER OF PRAYER

[Jesus said,] "Heaven and earth shall pass away:
but my words shall not pass away."

MARK 13:31 ASV

Is there true power in prayer? Sometimes when things get rough in life, prayer seems as though it is a menial task that will not get anything done. But when we pray, more happens than we can imagine.

Our prayers do more than fill an empty room. They do more than fill our minds with good thoughts. When we pray the Scriptures, all of Heaven prepares itself to fulfill the promises of God for your life. This means that everything God has spoken will come to pass on your behalf when the Word of God is spoken. His Word will outlast everything you see around you—the earth, the sky, and everything in between. It will never fail. It is settled in Heaven. And His Word tells us that He always causes us to triumph. It tells us that He is a healer. The words of the Scriptures tell us that God is a provider and that He is the one who strengthens us. The Word is so great that if the Author of it is for us, nothing can stand against us. When you pray the Word of God, Heaven and earth will be shaken before you ever find yourself in a place of loneliness and defeat.

Knowing this, you are assured victory in every area of your life. You have God's Word on it. One would ask, "Is there power in prayer?" The answer is yes, and more so. There is not just power, but there are countless promises from a faithful God.

WHERE IS THE LORD OF ELIJAH?

Elias was a man subject to like passions as we are, and he prayed earnestly that it might not rain: and it rained not on the earth by the space of three years and six months.

JAMES 5:17 KJV

My Creed leads me to think that prayer is efficacious, and surely a day's asking God to overrule all events for good is not lost. Still there is a great feeling that when a man is praying he's doing nothing, and this feeling makes us give undue importance to work, sometimes even to the hurrying over or even to the neglect of prayer.

Do not we rest in our day too much on the arm of flesh? Cannot the same wonders be done now as of old? Do not the eyes of the Lord run to and fro throughout the whole earth still to show himself strong on behalf of those who put their trust in Him? Oh that God would give me more practical faith in Him! Where is now the Lord God of Elijah? He is waiting for Elijah to call on Him.

-JAMES GILMOUR OF MONGOLIA, FROM E. M. BOUNDS,

When will we call upon God as they did in the days we read about in the Bible? So often, we want to see miracles, healing, and great works of God in biblical proportions, but we so often forget to seek His face in biblical proportions. God has not forsaken His people. Neither has He held back on His promises. He wants to live in us and work through us, if we allow Him.

Have we wasted precious hours of prayer in exchange for our own entrapments? Have the cares of this life overwhelmed us so greatly that there is little time left to pray? God still waits, eager for your company.

"Wherefore seeing we also are compassed about with so great a cloud of witnesses, let us lay aside every weight, and the sin which doth so easily beset us, and let us run with patience the race that is set before us, looking unto Jesus the author and finisher of our faith" (Hebrews 12:1-2 KJV).

God wants to be to you what He was to Elijah. He wants to show His faithfulness in the greatest victories and also in the times of greatest trouble. He wants us to lay aside the sin that holds us back from Him. He wants us to let go of our earthly burdens and enter into His love.

The Reason We Pray

*Thanks be to God, who gives us the victory
through our Lord Jesus Christ.*

1 Corinthians 15:57 nrsv

Have you ever wondered why we pray? What is it that moves individuals to get on their knees and appeal to a God they cannot see? Naturally, this may not seem to be the best way to live an overcoming life. It may not even appear to be worth the time that it takes to have such a conversation with someone who is invisible. But there is indeed something special about attaching ourselves to the unseen power of God.

We pray so that we can connect with God for a purpose, whether it is to accomplish something on this earth or to bring honor and praise to God as He listens to us. Prayer is the one power on this earth that cannot be defeated. It is immitigable. It cannot be conquered by any high authority. The highest authority, God, listens when His people appeal to Him.

Another reason we pray is so we can assure total victory in life. When you connect to God, you cannot be defeated. When the trials of life try to convict us, our appeal to God overwhelms those problems and replaces them with promises that cannot be broken. You can assure victory today if you connect with God through prayer.

DEPENDENT ON PRAYER

Pray without ceasing.

1 THESSALONIANS 5:17 KJV

We can live our lives totally dependent on prayer. We can do this because the One to whom we pray is utterly trustworthy. At face value, it seems impractical to think that we can pray nonstop, seeing that we have jobs, families, and other duties in life that call for attention. Yet our spiritual lifeblood flows through the veins of ceaseless prayer. As blood must constantly flow through our veins for us to survive, and as air must constantly enter our lungs for us to live, so must we always pray. But how do we pray without ceasing?

The Bible tells us that God will keep us in perfect peace if we continually keep our minds on Him. (See Isaiah 26:3.) This scripture holds the key as to how we pray without ceasing. When we keep our minds on God and His Word, He fills us with the power we need in order to strive in this life. With our minds continually on Him, we set ourselves into position to receive answers to the problems we face. We also have a constant source of joy, peace, and thanksgiving. This ceaseless prayer of keeping our mind stayed on Him is what we as Christians depend on in order to live.

Today, you can make it a point to pray without ceasing. You can keep your mind continually on God, and He will bless your life as you do.

FOUND IN HIM

Great is our Lord, and of great power: his understanding is infinite.

PSALM 147:5 KJV

My God! You are at once so great and so condescending, so high above the heavens and so accommodating to the misery of the creature, so infinite and so intimately enclosed in the depths of my heart, so terrible and so lovely, so jealous and so easy to be entreated of those who converse with You with the familiarity of pure love, when will Your children cease to be ignorant of You? Where shall I find a voice loud enough to reproach the whole world with its blindness, and tell it with authority all that You are? When we bid men look for You in their own hearts, it is as though we bade them search for You in the remotest and most unknown lands!

What territory is more distant or more unknown to the greater part of them, vain and dissipated as they are, than the ground of their own hearts? Do they ever know what it is to enter within themselves? Have they ever endeavored to find the way? Can they even form the most distant conception of the nature of that interior sanctuary, that impenetrable depth of the soul where You desire to be worshipped in spirit and in truth? They are ever outside of themselves in the objects of their ambition or of their pleasure. Alas! how can they understand heavenly truths, since, as our Lord says, they cannot even comprehend those which are earthly? (See John 3:12.) They cannot conceive what it is to enter within themselves by serious reflection; what would they say if they were bid to come out of themselves that they might be lost in God?

-FRANÇOIS FENELON

PSALM OF LIFE

To me to live is Christ, and to die is gain.

PHILIPPIANS 1:21 KJV

"There are two certanties in life—death and taxes!"

Have you ever heard that statement? It, and many like it, have stolen the zeal and joy of life from many. It is meant to tear down and discourage, rather than build up and encourage. God has given us a greater promise from His Word, one which gives true certainty beyond "death and taxes." He has given everlasting life to those who believe. Do you know what it means to have true life?

Life is real, life is earnest,
And the grave is not its goal.
Dust thou art, to dust returnest,
Was not spoken of the soul.

'Tis better, said a voice within
To bear the Christian's cross
Than sell this fleeting world for gold,
Which death shall prove but dross.

Far better when yon shriveled skies

Are like a banner furled,
To share in Christ's reproach than gain
The glory of the world.

Right is right since God is God
And right the day will win,
To doubt, would be disloyalty,
To falter would be sin.

-JOANNA P. MOORE

Let us never lose sight of the true meaning of life—Christ. If we hold on tight to Him, we will have embraced everything we will ever need to make life worth while.

A Whole Burnt Offering

Let my prayer be set forth before thee as incense;
and the lifting up of my hands as the evening sacrifice.

PSALM 141:2 KJV

There is scarce any one who desires to serve God, but does so for selfish reasons; we expect gain and not loss, consolation and not suffering, riches and not poverty, increase and not diminution. But the whole interior work is of an opposite character; to be lost, sacrificed, made less than nothing, and despoiled of an excessive delight, even in the gifts of God, that we may be forced to cling to Him alone.

We are like a patient eagerly desiring returning health, who feels his own pulse forty times a day, and requires his physician to prescribe frequent doses of various remedies, and to give him a daily assurance that he is getting better. Such is almost the only use we make of our spiritual conductors. We travel in a little round of everyday virtues, never gathering sufficient courage to pass generously beyond it, and our guides, like the doctor, flatter, console, encourage and strengthen our selfish sensitiveness, and administer pleasant remedies, to the effects of which we soon become insensible.

The moment we find ourselves deprived of the delights of grace, that milk for babes, we are at once in despair; a manifest proof that we were looking to the means, instead of to the end, and solely for selfish gratification.

Privations are meat for men; by them the soul is rendered hardy, is separated from self, and offered in a pure sacrifice to God; but we give up all, the moment they commence. We cannot but think that everything is going to ruin, when, in fact, the foundations are just beginning to be solidly laid. Nothing would give us more delight than that God should do all his pleasure with us, provided it should always be to magnify and perfect us in our own eyes. But if we are not willing to be destroyed and annihilated, we shall never become that whole burnt offering, which is entirely consumed in the blaze of God's love.

We desire to enter into a state of pure faith, and retain our own wisdom! To be a babe, and great in our own eyes! Ah! What a sad delusion!

-FRANÇOIS FENELON

How to Become Wholly God's

According to my earnest expectation and my hope,
that in nothing I shall be ashamed, but that with all boldness,
as always, so now also Christ shall be magnified in my body,
whether it be by life, or by death.

PHILIPPIANS 1:20 KJV

Having found in many books different methods of going to God, and divers practices of the spiritual life, I thought this would serve rather to puzzle me, than facilitate what I sought after, which was nothing but how to become wholly God's.

This made me resolve to give the all for the All: so after having given myself wholly to God, to make all the satisfaction I could for my sins, I renounced, for the love of Him, everything that was not He; and I began to live as if there was none but He and I in the world. Sometimes I considered myself before Him as a poor criminal at the feet of his judge; at other times I beheld Him in my heart as my Father, as my God: I worshiped Him the oftenest that I could, keeping my mind in His holy Presence, and recalling it as often as I found it wandered from Him. I found no small pain in this exercise, and yet I continued it, notwithstanding all the difficulties that occurred, without troubling or disquieting myself when my mind had wandered involuntarily. I made this my business, as much all the day long as at the appointed times of prayer; for at all times, every hour, every minute, even in the height of my business, I drove away from my mind everything that was capable of interrupting my thought of God.

-BROTHER LAWRENCE

TO THE GLORY OF GOD

*Whether therefore ye eat, or drink, or whatsoever ye do,
do all to the glory of God.*

1 CORINTHIANS 10:31 KJV

Serving God involves more than just our praying and service in church. It involves every aspect of our lives. As Christians, we have the sacred honor of being God's servants in this earth. But clearly, not all of us are preachers and church leaders. Some of us are business owners, secretaries, doctors, or housewives. We vary greatly in our occupations. But did you know that we can accomplish our occupation for the glory of God? Our service to God can be the work we do every day, if we dedicate it to Him and allow that work to properly represent Him. This is what William Law wrote about in his *Serious Call to a Devout and Holy Life*:

Now let any one but find out the reason why he is to be thus strictly pious in his prayer, and he will find the same as strong a reason to be as strictly pious in all the other parts of his life. For there is not the least shadow of a reason why we should make God the rule and measure of our prayers; why we should then look wholly unto Him, and pray according to His will; but what equally proves it necessary for us to look wholly unto God, and make Him the rule and measure of all the other actions of our life.

-WILLIAM LAW

If our everyday activities—including our work—reflect a prayerful person, then everything we do will be done well. We will be known as people of excellence—diligent in our work. Our lives will constantly be open to promotion and blessings. And most of all, God will be honored in everything we do.

Rest and Believe

*Through faith we understand that the worlds were framed by
the word of God, so that things which are seen were not made of
things which do appear.*

HEBREWS 11:3 KJV

God made everything, out of nothing! The thought that
such a feat could be possible will boggle even the most scientific mind. Yet, God made everything in this manner. Knowing
such to be true, our doubts in His ability to provide for us
should now come to rest, for even though you may have nothing at all right now, God has everything He needs in order to
provide for you. Our doubts need not only rest, but we, also.
We must lay aside our worries and give ourselves to suitable
devotion. It is time to rest and believe.

I believe, O God, that thou art an eternal, incomprehensible spirit, infinite in all perfections, who didst make all things
out of nothing, and dost govern them all by thy wise providence.

Let me always adore thee with profound humility, as my
Sovereign Lord; and help me to love and praise thee with godlike affections, and suitable devotion.

-RICHARD ALLEN

Two Simple Words

[God said,] "He who offers a sacrifice of thanksgiving honors Me;
and to him who orders his way aright I shall show the
salvation of God."

PSALM 50:23 NASB

Have you ever come to God in times of trouble, only to realize how long it has been since you last prayed? Most of us can relate. So often, it is easy to remember to run into His loving arms when we need Him, but never to take the time to say "Thank You."

Yet, it is these two simple words that honor God more than most anything else we can pray. It is counted as worship. When we remember God, we affirm that He is the One who gets the credit for every good thing in our lives.

In the Bible, the Lord is likened to a man of war, but this comparison is true in more ways than one.

God and a soldier all men do adore
In time of war, and not before;
When the war is over, and all things righted,
God is forgotten, and the soldier slighted.

-RICHARD ALLEN

God wants us to remember Him once the war is over. He desires that we stand to worship Him when the battle is won. Let us never forget about the one who "always causes us to triumph." Let us never forget to say "thank You" to the One who wakes us up in the morning and gives us rest at night. Let us never forget the One who puts food on our table and clothes on our back. All He desires are two simple words. All He wants is for us to say "Thank You."

LET TEMPTATION DRIVE
YOU TO HIM

*I take pleasure in infirmities, in reproaches, in necessities,
in persecutions, in distresses for Christ's sake: for when I am weak,
then am I strong.*

2 CORINTHIANS 12:10 KJV

The following is a story of a slave who, even in the most
adverse of circumstance, learned what many of us must learn
of today—the power of God's grace.

I labored one year under these distressing temptations,
when it pleased God to give me another offer of mercy. In
1784, I, along with sixteen other persons, worked for Mrs.
Robinson; all of them were devoted to God, except myself
and two others. The divine presence was with these men, and
every night and morning they kept a prayer meeting, and read
some portion of Scripture. On the fifth of January, as one of
them was reading the Parable of the Sower, the word came
with power to my heart. I stood up and desired him to explain
the parable; and while he was showing me the meaning of it, I
was deeply convinced that I was one of the stony ground
hearers. When I considered how many offers of mercy I had
abused from day to day, and how many convictions I had tri-

fled away, I was astonished that the Lord had borne with me so long. I was at the same time truly thankful that he gave me a desire to return to him, and resolved by the grace of God to set out afresh for the kingdom of Heaven.

As my convictions increased, so did my desires after the Lord and in order to keep them alive, I resolved to make a covenant with him in the most solemn manner I was able. For this purpose I went into the garden at midnight, and kneeled down upon the snow, lifting up my hands, eyes, and heart to Heaven; and entreated the Lord, who had called me by his Holy Spirit out of ignorance and wickedness, that he would increase and strengthen my awakenings and desires, and impress my heart with the importance of eternal things; and that I might never find rest or peace again, till I found peace with him, and received a seine of his pardoning love. The Lord mercifully looked down upon me, and gave me such a sight of my fallen state that I plainly saw, without an interest in Christ, and an application of his atoning blood to my conscience, I should be lost to all eternity. This led me to a diligent use of all the means of Grace, and to forsake and renounce everything that I knew to be sinful.

The more convictions increased, and the more I felt the wickedness of my own heart; yet the Lord helped me to strive against evil, so that temptations instead of prevailing against me, drove me nearer to him.

-BOSTON KING

God's grace will draw you nearer to Him, not further from Him. No matter how great the sin, or how bad the thought, God is interested in restoring you and bringing you to himself. He will not, for any reason, cast you away if you call upon Him.

ONE GOD

There are three that bear record in heaven, the Father, the Word,
and the Holy Ghost: and these three are one.

1 JOHN 5:7 KJV

These three are one—the shell, the yoke, the white.
Together, they are an egg. One part is no more an egg than the
other. Neither are they three eggs, when viewed separately.
They are all equally one egg, whether together or separate.
This is also true of God, who is Father, Son, and Holy Spirit.
No part of this Holy trinity is exempt from being God.
Neither is any part any more or less divine than the other. To
say "Father, Son, and Holy Spirit" does not give notice to
three Gods, but one.

I believe that in the unity of the Godhead there is a trinity
of persons, that thou art perfectly one and perfectly three; one
essence and three persons. I believe, O blessed Jesus, that thou
art of one substance with the father, the very and eternal God,
that thou didst take upon thee our frail nature, that thou
didst truly suffer, and wert crucified, dead and buried, to rec-
oncile us to thy Father, and to be a sacrifice for sin.

-RICHARD ALLEN

God laid aside His majesty in order to connect with sinful men, in the person of Jesus Christ. Because of this sacrifice, we can now commune with Him without sin, with the Holy Spirit living inside of us. Today, we have perfect fellowship with the Father, the Son, and the Holy Spirit—one God.

SHOUT HIS PRAISES AS YOU GO

The Lamb which is in the midst of the throne shall feed them, and
shall lead them unto living fountains of waters: and God shall wipe
away all tears from their eyes.

REVELATION 7:17 KJV

This life will see no happiness as great as the joy we will
see when we are finished with our journey on this earth. No
matter how rough things often seem, there is one fact that
cannot be changed by circumstances—you will see Heaven
one day if you belong to Jesus Christ. John Jasper clearly
understood this hope as he passionately preached to all who
would listen.

Our eyes go far beyond the smaller stars, our home is clear
out of sight of the twinkling orbs. The chariot that will come
to take us to our Father's mansion will sweep out by the flick-
ering lights, and never halt, till it brings us in clear view of the
throne of the Lamb. Don't hitch your hopes to the sun or the
stars. Your home has got Jesus for its light, and your hopes
must travel in that way. Nothing short of the pearly gates will
satisfy me, and I charge you, my people, to fix your feet on the
solid Rock, your hearts on Calvary, and your eyes on the
Throne of the Lamb. These strifes and griefs will soon be

over. We shall see the King in His glory and be at ease. Go on, go on, ye ransomed of the Lord. Shout His praises as you go.

-JOHN JASPER

Even if there is nothing left to shout and rejoice about in your life on this earth, there is an assurance that will remain unchanged—the glory of Heaven. Shout His praises as you get closer to that day. Rejoice, knowing that your eternity will be gloriously everlasting, in sharp contrast to this short and often troublesome life. Forever, you will be in His presence, never to see grief, poverty, or hatred again. That great day is coming, and it cannot be stopped. Shout His praises as you go.

CALLED ACCORDING TO HIS PURPOSE

We know that all things work together for good to them that love God, to them who are the called according to his purpose.

ROMANS 8:28 KJV

As Christians, we are called according to His purpose. This means that all of us have a reason for being here, no matter what stage of life in which we find ourselves. Whether young or old, rich or poor, we all have a reason to live this life the way God wants us to live.

For this reason, we ought to always lift our voices in adoration of Him, because everything we see in life will work together for good. It may not seem as though things are good on their own, but one day, in retrospect, we will look back from the glory and splendor of Heaven and realize that it was worth it all.

> *I praise Him for both smile and frown,*
> *And for the gain and loss*
> *I praise Him for the future crown,*
> *And for the present Cross.*
>
> *I praise Him for the storm cloud*

That drove me trembling to His breast,
And for this strange—this settled peace—
Which nothing can destroy."

-JOANNA P. MOORE

It is worth it all when we praise God. Today, can you make a commitment to praise God, no matter what you face?

GOD'S CHOSEN

[Jesus said,] "Many are called, but few are chosen."

MATTHEW 22:14 KJV

"When God has a work to be executed, he also chooses the man to execute it. He also qualifies the workman for the work."—Daniel Alexander Payne, in declining the offer for the position of public lecturer for the Anti-Slavery Committee

Many are called, but few are chosen. Why? Because so few allow God to qualify them. Very often, those who are called are not even able to do the thing for which they are called. This is why the apostle Paul stated:

"Ye see your calling, brethren, how that not many wise men after the flesh, not many mighty, not many noble, are called: But God hath chosen the foolish things of the world to confound the wise; and God hath chosen the weak things of the world to confound the things which are mighty; and base things of the world, and things which are despised, hath God chosen, yea, and things which are not, to bring to nought things that are: That no flesh should glory in his presence" (1 Corinthians 1:26-29 KJV).

God is the qualifier, not man. We ourselves, do not even

qualify our own selves. This way, God gets the glory for every true success in our lives, and no flesh (nothing independent of God) shall have the right to attain praise except our Savior.

When God qualifies you, He gives you the divine right to accomplish the work He has for you. Your success is assured because your qualifier has called you.

MARCH TILL VICTORY IS WON

I press toward the mark for the prize of the high calling of God in Christ Jesus.

PHILIPPIANS 3:14 KJV

One day, you will see that at the end of the race you are running is a prize that words cannot describe. The prize you will hold will not be a temporal trophy that sits on your mantle. It will be an everlasting reward. It will be a crown that will let everyone know that although life on this earth had many trials, you pressed on and made it through the gates of pearls.

In the meantime, isn't it good to know that your heart can hold such a glorious assurance? You can now continue your race, and you can, as the poet James Weldon Johnson once wrote:

> *Lift every voice and sing,*
> *Till earth and heaven ring,*
> *Ring with the harmonies of Liberty;*
> *Let our rejoicing rise*
> *High as the listening skies,*
> *Let it resound loud as the rolling sea.*
> *Sing a song full of the faith that*
> *the dark past has taught us,*

Sing a song full of the hope
that the present has brought us,
Facing the rising sun
of our new day begun,
Let us march on till victory is won.

-JAMES WELDON JOHNSON

LET US REMEMBER

Samuel took a stone, and set it between Mizpeh and Shen,
and called the name of it Ebenezer, saying,
Hitherto hath the Lord helped us.

1 SAMUEL 7:12 KJV

God of our weary years,
God of our silent tears,
Thou who has brought us thus far on the way;
Thou who has by Thy might
Led us into the light,
Keep us forever in the path, we pray.
Lest our feet stray from the places,
our God, where we met Thee,
Lest, our hearts drunk with the
wine of the world, we forget Thee;
Shadowed beneath Thy hand,
May we forever stand.
True to our God,
True to our native land.

-JAMES WELDON JOHNSON

We have heard it said, "I'm black and proud." And yes, we
ought to be appreciative of who God has made us. But let us
remember that it was God who helped us. He is our

Ebenezer—our Stone of help. Let us not allow our hearts to be "drunk with the wine of the world," lest we forget God and think that our own strength and ability has gotten us this far. We can accomplish more with God on a bad day than the best minds in the world can accomplish on their best day. But it is the Lord, our Ebenezer, our Stone of help, who has indeed helped us.

Look back and see how much He has taught us and how great a distance He has brought us. Where, less than two centuries ago our ancestors were slaves, today we are exploring space, running governments, leading the largest corporations in the world, and telling the world about a resurrected Savior. It is only God who could have brought us this far. Let us remember.

FIX OUR HOPES ON HIGH

[Jesus said,] "Seek first His kingdom and His righteousness, and all
these things will be added to you."

MATTHEW 6:33 NASB

I *pity those who seek no more*
Than such a world can give;
Wretched they are, and blind, and poor,
And dying while they live.
Since sin has filled the earth with woe,
And creatures fade and die;
Lord wean our hearts from things below,
And fix our hopes on high.

-JOHN NEWTON

Fix our hopes on high.

What would happen if everything you did from this day
forward was for the glory of God? What would happen if such
things were beyond your ability and only for His good pleasure? How greatly would your life have changed?

This world has no shortage of distractions. We are daily
surrounded by entertainment and pleasures of this world. So
much, in fact, that our entire day and evening could easily be

filled with all that this world has to offer. Sadly, many Christians spend their entire days and evenings entrapped in this very thing. Can we survive without our entrapments? Will we ever overcome our constant quest for riches?

We will please God only when we can go to Him in faith, having forsaken all the things of this world in exchange for the things that only He can give us. Today, are you willing to lay hold on all that God has in store for you?

HIS BLOOD HAS PAID
YOUR DEBT

You give us victory over our enemies, you put our adversaries to shame.

PSALM 44:7 NIV

Did you know that we win every battle and proclaim victory in every trial? We have that right because God always causes us to be victorious. We win because Jesus has won for us. Because of Him, we no longer have to go through life the way we used to. We can now live on, fully relying on His strength and power to take us through every day.

Once perishing in blood I lay,
Creatures no help could give,
But Jesus passed me in the way,
He saw, and bid me live.
Though Satan still his rule maintained,
And all his arts employed;
That mighty Word his rage restrained,
I could not be destroyed.
At length the time of love arrived
When I my Lord should know,
Then Satan, of his pow'r deprived,

Was forced to let me go.
O can I e'er that day forget
When Jesus kindly spoke!
"Poor soul, my blood has paid thy debt,
And now I break thy yoke.
Henceforth I take thee for my own,
And give myself to thee;
Forsake the idols thou hast known,
And yield thyself to me."

-JOHN NEWTON

OUR PRESENT DIFFICULTY

I reckon that the sufferings of this present time are not worthy to be compared with the glory which shall be revealed in us.

ROMANS 8:18 KJV

I can only imagine the choices that were before the former president of the United States. His country was falling apart and was facing the prospect of a war that could potentially take the lives of countless fathers and sons. Then, war began as the first fires were shot from the Confederate Fort Multrie against Fort Sumpter. After a spirited return fire, total war had begun, and the president, having been in office for only a month, had more demands upon his leadership than ever.

Have you ever faced a time of difficulty where unimaginable demands were made of you? In what way do you believe the issue could have been better resolved? President Lincoln had one way in particular, and we can glean from it today.

Intelligence, patriotism, Christianity and a firm reliance on Him, who has never yet forsaken this favored land, are still competent to adjust in the best way, all our present difficulty.

-ABRAHAM LINCOLN
INAUGURAL ADDRESS, 1861

Just as the newly appointed president during the Civil War, we also have a way out from being overwhelmed. That way out is a firm reliance on God. He is the only one who cares enough for us to take our burdens and make them His own. Then, when He takes our troubles as His own, He fills us with His peace. How do we handle our present difficulty? By understanding that peace is only a prayer away.

STRENGTH THROUGH PRAYER

[The Lord saith,] Let the people renew their strength.

ISAIAH 41:1 KJV

All things on earth need to be renewed. No created thing continueth by itself. "Thou renewest the face of the year," was the Psalmist's utterance. Even the trees, which wear not themselves with care, nor shorten their lives with labour, must drink of the rain of heaven and suck from the hidden treasures of the soil. The cedars of Lebanon, which God has planted, only live because day by day they are full of sap fresh drawn from the earth. Neither can man's life be sustained without renewal from God. As it is necessary to repair the waste of the body by the frequent meal, so we must repair the waste of the soul by feeding upon the Book of God, or by listening to the preached Word, or by the soul-fattening table of the ordinances. How depressed are our graces when means are neglected! What poor starvelings some saints are who live without the diligent use of the Word of God and secret prayer!

If our piety can live without God it is not of divine creating; it is but a dream; for if God had begotten it, it would wait upon Him as the flowers wait upon the dew. Without constant restoration we are not ready for the perpetual assaults of hell, or the stern afflictions of heaven, or even for the strifes within. When the whirlwind shall be loosed, woe to the tree that hath not sucked up fresh sap, and grasped the rock with many intertwisted roots. When tempests arise, woe to the mariners that have not strengthened their mast, nor cast their anchor, nor sought the haven.

If we suffer the good to grow weaker, the evil will surely gather strength and struggle desperately for the mastery over us; and so, mayhap, a painful desolation, and a lamentable disgrace may follow. Let us draw near to the footstool of divine mercy in humble entreaty, and we shall realize the fulfillment of the promise, "They that wait on the Lord shall renew their strength."

-CHARLES HADDON SPURGEON

It's in Your Hands

I press toward the mark for the prize of the high calling of God in Christ Jesus.

PHILIPPIANS 3:14 KJV

An old man was very wise, and he could answer questions that were almost impossible for most people to answer. So, two young people went to him one day and said, "We're going to trick this guy today. We're going to catch a bird and carry it to this old man. And we're going to ask him, 'This which we hold in our hands today, is it alive or dead?' If he says 'dead,' we're going to turn it loose and let it fly. But if he says 'alive,' we're going to crush it." So, they walked up to this old man, and they said, "This that we hold in our hands today, is it alive, or is it dead?" He looked at the young people, and he smiled and said, "It's in your hands."

-FANNIE LOU HAMER

There is something precious in your hands today. And it is your choice whether it will live or die. That precious thing is the call upon your life—the very reason you were born. Sadly, few people ever fully recognize their potential in this life and cross their finish line with unwritten books, unsung songs, and unfulfilled dreams.

Whether you are Black, Asian, White, or any other race, you have a special purpose on this earth. That purpose left unfulfilled can hold back blessings from those who need them most.

As Christians, we are not on this earth to be served, but to serve. We are here to boldly be who God has called us to be. Whether you are called to be a minister or a janitor, doing things God's way can change the world. Many people who were once viewed as insignificant became passionate about what they did, and they changed the world. These people knew that the destiny that was before them had only one hindrance, and that hindrance was the choice to do nothing.

What is your choice today? Do you dare do nothing with what is in your hands? Or, will you, as so many of your forefathers, go forward into all that you are called to? There are potentially millions of people waiting for you to change their life with your calling. How long will they wait?

Today is your day to take what is in your hands and go forward with everything God has put in you. This is the day to begin functioning through God's ability. Then, no matter what your occupation, you can make an impact on this world that cannot be forgotten.

The Master's Work

*My beloved brethren, be ye stedfast, unmoveable, always abounding
in the work of the Lord, forasmuch as ye know that your labour is
not in vain in the Lord.*

1 Corinthians 15:58 KJV

Sometimes serving God can be a hard thing to do. It involves a lot of work, as well as prayer. It involves taking the best of us and using it to the fullest, all while laying aside our desires in exchange for God's perfect will. But more than any other thing, doing the work of God has rewards that will enrich your spirit and cause you to spiritually mature. After all our toil is done in this world, we will see that it was worth it all. Perhaps the poem below says it best:

*Where hast been toiling all day, sweet heart,
That thy brow is burdened and sad;
The Master's work may make weary feet,
But it leaves the spirit glad.*

*Is thy curse of comfort failing?
Rise and share it with another
And through all the years of famine
It will serve thee and thy brother.
Scanty fare for one
Makes ample feast for two.*

-Joanna P. Moore

God gives us the ability to minister to others, even when we are at the end of our own ability. If you are feeling burned out today, go encourage someone. Go bless another brother or sister. Take the burden off of them, and God will remove the burdens from your life.

What Will Happen to Him?

Some have compassion, making a difference.

JUDE 22 KJV

Will your compassion make a difference in someone else's life today? It can, if you let it happen. The compassion of Martin Luther King Jr. changed the lives of millions because he let it happen through him. During his life and ministry, he gave the following sermon that spoke of the importance of compassion. Let it speak to your heart today.

One day a man came to Jesus; and he wanted to raise some questions about some vital matters in life. At points, he wanted to trick Jesus and show him that he knew a little more than Jesus knew, and through this, throw him off base. Now that question could have easily ended up in a philosophical and theological debate.

But Jesus immediately pulled that question from midair and placed it on a dangerous curve between Jerusalem and Jericho. And he talked about a certain man, who fell among thieves. You remember that a Levite and a priest passed by on the other side. They didn't stop to help him. And finally a man of another race came by. He got down from his beast, decided not to be compassionate by proxy, but instead, admin-

istered first aid, and helped the man in need. Jesus ended up
saying, this was the good man, this was the great man,
because he had the capacity to project the "I" into the "thou,"
and to be concerned about his brother.

Now you know, we use our imagination a great deal to try
to determine why the priest and the Levite didn't stop. At
times we say they were busy going to a church meeting—an
ecclesiastical gathering—and they had to get on down to
Jerusalem, so they wouldn't be late for their meeting. At other
times we would speculate that there was a religious law that
"one who was engaged in religious ceremonials was not to
touch a human body twenty-four hours before the ceremony."
And every now and then we begin to wonder whether maybe
they were not going down to Jerusalem, or down to Jericho,
rather to organize a "Jericho Road Improvement Association."
That's a possibility. Maybe they felt that it was better to deal
with the problem from the causal root, rather than to get
bogged down with an individual effort.

But I'm going to tell you what my imagination tells me.
It's possible that these men were afraid. You see, the Jericho
road is a dangerous road. I remember when Mrs. King and I
were first in Jerusalem. We rented a car and drove from
Jerusalem down to Jericho. And as soon as we got on that
road, I said to my wife, "I can see why Jesus used this as a set-
ting for his parable." It's a winding, meandering road. It's really
conducive for ambushing. You start out in Jerusalem, which is
about 1200 miles, or rather 1200 feet above sea level. And by
the time you get down to Jericho, fifteen or twenty minutes

later, you're about 2200 feet below sea level. That's a dangerous road. In the days of Jesus it came to be known as the
"Bloody Pass." And you know, it's possible that the priest and
the Levite looked over that man on the ground and wondered
if the robbers were still around. Or it's possible that they felt
that the man on the ground was merely faking. And he was
acting like he had been robbed and hurt, in order to seize
them over there, lure them there for quick and easy seizure.
And so the first question that the Levite asked was, "If I stop
to help this man, what will happen to me?" But then the Good
Samaritan came by. And he reversed the question: "If I do not
stop to help this man, what will happen to him?"

-MARTIN LUTHER KING JR.
SPEECH, "I'VE BEEN TO THE MOUNTAINTOP," 1968

Your compassion makes a difference. There are many out
there waiting for your generosity and encouragement. Perhaps
you are desiring such generosity and encouragement yourself.
It is possible that God will bless you with the greatest and
most compassionate people, if you become the very thing you
desire.

TRUE DISCIPLES

[Jesus said,] "Herein is my Father glorified, that ye bear much fruit;
so shall ye be my disciples."

JOHN 15:8 KJV

Are those who do not bear much fruit not disciples? They
may be, but in a backward and immature stage. Of those who
bear much fruit, Christ says: "These are My disciples, such as
I would have them be—these are true disciples." Just as we say
of someone in whom the idea of manliness is realized: "That
is a man!" So our Lord tells who are disciples after His heart,
worthy of the name: those who bear much fruit. We find this
double sense of the word "disciple" in the Gospel. Sometimes
it is applied to all who accepted Christ's teaching. At other
times it includes only the inner circle of those who followed
Christ wholly and gave themselves to His training for service.
The difference has existed throughout all ages. There have
always been a smaller number of God's people who have
sought to serve Him with their whole heart, while the majority have been content with a very small measure of the knowledge of His grace and will.

And what is the difference between this smaller inner circle and the many who do not seek admission to it? We find it
in the words: much fruit. With many Christians the thought
of personal safety, which at their first awakening, was a legiti-

mate one, remains to the end the one aim of their religion. The idea of service and fruit is always a secondary and very subordinate one. The honest longing for much fruit does not trouble them. Souls that have heard the call to live wholly for their Lord, to give their lives for Him as He gave His for them, can never be satisfied with this. Their cry is to bear as much fruit as they possibly can, as much as their Lord ever can desire or give in them.

Bear much fruit: so shall ye be My disciples—Let me beg every reader to consider these words most seriously. Be not content with the thought of gradually doing a little more or better work. In this way it may never come. Take the words, much fruit, as the revelation of your heavenly Vine of what you must be, of what you can be. Accept fully the impossibility, the utter folly of attempting it in your strength. Let the words call you to look anew upon the Vine, an undertaking to live out its heavenly fullness in you. Let them waken in you once again the faith and the confession: "I am a branch of the true Vine; I can bear much fruit to His glory and the glory of the Father."

We need not judge others. But we see in God's Word everywhere two classes of disciples. Let there be no hesitation as to where we take our place. Let us ask Him to reveal to us how He asks and claims a life wholly given up to Him, to be as full of His Spirit as He can make us. Let our desire be nothing less than perfect cleansing, unbroken abiding, closest communion, abundant fruitfulness—true branches of the true Vine.

-ANDREW MURRAY

DID HE SUFFER IN VAIN?

[Christ] was wounded for our transgressions, he was bruised
for our iniquities: the chastisement of our peace was upon him;
and with his stripes we are healed.

ISAIAH 53:5 KJV

Shall we look upon His sufferings and still doubt in our hearts? Did He suffer in vain? Did He carry His cross up Golgotha's hill, only to hold back on His promise? Of course not. Then why do we so often lose faith? Why do we so often close our eyes to the crucified Jesus? If we look only to Him and appropriate the power of the blood He shed, we will never, ever lose our hope.

O, my God! In all my dangers temporal and spiritual I will hope in You who are Almighty power, and therefore able to relieve me; who are infinite goodness, and therefore ready and willing to assist me.

O precious blood of my dear Redeemer! O gaping wounds of my crucified Saviour! Who can contemplate the sufferings of God incarnate, and not raise his hope, and not put his trust in Him. What though my body be crumbled into dust, and that dust blown over the face of the earth, yet I undoubtedly know my Redeemer lives, and shall raise me up at the last day; whether I am comforted or left desolate;

whether I enjoy peace or am afflicted with temptations, whether I am healthful or sickly, succored or abandoned by the good things of this life, I will always hope in You, O my chiefest, infinite good.

-RICHARD ALLEN

I WILL HELP THEE

I will help thee, saith the Lord.

ISAIAH 41:14 KJV

This morning let us hear the Lord Jesus speak to each one of us: "I will help thee." "It is but a small thing for Me, thy God, to help thee. Consider what I have done already. What! Not help thee? Why, I bought thee with My blood. What! Not help thee? I have died for thee; and if I have done the greater, will I not do the less? Help thee! It is the least thing I will ever do for thee; I have done more, and will do more.

"Before the world began I chose thee. I made the covenant for thee. I laid aside My glory and became a man for thee; I gave up My life for thee; and if I did all this, I will surely help thee now. In helping thee, I am giving thee what I have bought for thee already. If thou hadst need of a thousand times as much help, I would give it thee; thou requirest little compared with what I am ready to give. 'Tis much for thee to need, but it is nothing for me to bestow. 'Help thee?' Fear not! If there were an ant at the door of thy granary asking for help, it would not ruin thee to give him a handful of thy wheat; and thou art nothing but a tiny insect at the door of My all-sufficiency. 'I will help thee.'"

O my soul, is not this enough? Dost thou need more

strength than the omnipotence of the United Trinity? Dost thou want more wisdom than exists in the Father, more love than displays itself in the Son, or more power than is manifest in the influences of the Spirit? Bring hither thine empty pitcher! Surely this well will fill it. Haste, gather up thy wants, and bring them here—thine emptiness, thy woes, thy needs. Behold, this river of God is full for thy supply; what canst thou desire beside? Go forth, my soul, in this thy might. The Eternal God is thine helper!

Fear not, I am with thee, oh, be not dismay'd!

I, I am thy God, and will still give thee aid.

-CHARLES HADDON SPURGEON

THE HUSBANDMAN

[Jesus said,] "My Father is the husbandman."

JOHN 15:1 KJV

A vine must have a husbandman to plant and watch over it, to receive and rejoice in its fruit. Jesus says: "My Father is the husbandman." He was "the vine of God's planting." All He was and did, He owed to the Father; in all He only sought the Father's will and glory. He had become man to show us what a creature ought to be to its Creator. He took our place, and the spirit of His life before the Father was ever what He seeks to make ours: "Of him, and through him, and to him are all things." He became the true Vine, that we might be true branches. Both in regard to Christ and ourselves, the words teach us the two lessons of absolute dependence and perfect confidence.

My Father is the Husbandman—Christ ever lived in the spirit of what He once said: "The Son can do nothing of himself." As dependent as a vine is on a husbandman for the place where it is to grow, for its fencing in and watering and pruning. Christ felt himself entirely dependent on the Father every day for the wisdom and the strength to do the Father's will. As He said in John 14:10: "The words that I say unto you, I speak not from Myself; but the Father abiding in Me doeth his works." This absolute dependence had as its blessed counterpart the most blessed confidence that He had nothing to fear: the Father could not disappoint Him. With such a Husbandman as His Father, He could enter death and the grave. He could trust God to raise Him up. All that Christ is and has, He has, not in himself, but from the Father.

My Father is the Husbandman. That is as blessedly true for us as for Christ. Christ is about to teach His disciples about their being branches. Before He ever uses the word, or speaks at all of abiding in Him or bearing fruit, He turns their eyes heavenward to the Father watching over them, and working all in them. At the very root of all Christian life lies the thought that God is to do all, that our work is to give and leave ourselves in His hands, in the confession of utter helplessness and dependence, in the assured confidence that He gives all we need. The great lack of the Christian life is that, even where we trust Christ, we leave God out of the count. Christ came to bring us to God. Christ lived the life of a man exactly as we have to live it. Christ the Vine points to God the Husbandman. As He trusted God, let us trust God, that everything we ought to be and have, as those who belong to the Vine, will be given us from above.

Isaiah said: "A vineyard of red wine. I the Lord do keep it; I will water it every moment: lest any hurt it, I will keep it night and day" (Isaiah 27:2-3 KJV). Ere we begin to think of fruit or branches, let us have our heart filled with the faith: as glorious as the Vine, is the Husbandman. As high and holy as is our calling, so mighty and loving is the God who will work it all. As surely as the Husbandman made the Vine what it was to be, will He make each branch what it is to be. Our Father is our Husbandman, the Surety for our growth and fruit.

Blessed Father, we are Thy husbandry. Oh, that Thou mayest have honor of the work of Thy hands! O my Father, I desire to open my heart to the joy of this wondrous truth: My Father is the Husbandman. Teach me to know and trust Thee, and to see that the same deep interest with which Thou caredst for and delightedst in the Vine, extends to every branch, to me too.

-ANDREW MURRAY

O BLACK AND UNKNOWN BARDS

Faith is the substance of things hoped for, the evidence of things not seen. For by it the elders obtained a good report.

HEBREWS 11:1-2 KJV

There is a wide, wide wonder in it all,
That from degraded rest and servile toil
The fiery spirit of the seer should call
These simple children of the sun and soil.

O black slave singers, gone, forgot, unfamed,
You—you alone, of all the long, long line
Of those who've sung untaught, unknown, unnamed,
Have stretched out upward, seeking the divine.

You sang not deeds of heroes or of kings;
No chant of bloody war, no exulting paean
No arms-won triumphs; but your humble strings
You touched in chord with music empyrean.

You sang far better than you knew; the songs
That for your listeners' hungry hearts sufficed
Still live—but more than this to you belongs:

You sang a race from wood and stone to Christ.

-JAMES WELDON JOHNSON

Today, you are somebody because someone made sacrifices for you. Perhaps there is nothing on earth more hopeful, more beautiful, yet more tearful than the song of the slave.

Uneducated they were, yet only because their minds were caged by the bondage they suffered. Weak they were, but only because of the toil and hardship they endured. But their spirits were strong. And from these spirits were lifted up songs of praise to the God of all the earth.

We must never forget to honor God for such precious saints. For, though they suffered bondage, their cries to God never went unanswered.

Have you ever wondered what ever happened to the old mother who died in the cotton fields? Or the young man who was lynched for merely being black? Have you wondered what ever happened to the young woman who died giving birth to a child conceived in the shame of rape? And what of the old man who died of fatigue, when his days could go no further?

All of these, those who called upon the name of the Lord were saved. Today, their past toil has been long forgotten. For, with open arms, they were received by our Savior in Heaven. With open arms, they were embraced, some for the very first time. Mothers are reunited with their lost children. Men are reunited with their wives who were sold away. Children have long reunited with their siblings and friends who were lost under the hopelessness and bondage of slavery. To them, the struggle is over.

They will never hunger again, neither shall they thirst. God has wiped away every tear from their eyes. The tribulation they endured on this earth has been replaced with everlasting life in the presence of God.

Will you see them someday? Will you see Christ? Will you also enter the very gates of your ancestors, and walk into God's Heaven? Will you give your life to Jesus, just as they did? With them in Heaven are people of all races and nationalities. Are you willing to share eternal life with them also? Today, if you ask Him to come into your heart, He will abide with you and give you eternal life. Then you will see those who went before you. And most of all, you will see Jesus, your Savior, face to face.

THE CLEANSING

[Jesus said,] "Every branch in me that beareth not fruit he
taketh away: and every branch that beareth fruit, he purgeth it,
that it may bring forth more fruit."

JOHN 15:2 KJV

There are two remarkable things about the vine. There is not a plant of which the fruit has so much spirit in it, of which spirit can be so abundantly distilled as the vine. And there is not a plant, which so soon runs into wild wood, that hinders its fruit, and therefore needs the most merciless pruning. I look out of my window here on large vineyards: the chief care of the vinedresser is the pruning. You may have a trellis vine rooting so deep in good soil that it needs neither digging, nor fertilizing, nor watering: pruning it cannot dispense with, if it is to bear good fruit. Some trees need occasional pruning; others bear perfect fruit without any: the vine must have it. And so our Lord tells us, here at the very outset of the parable, that the one work the Father does to the branch that bears fruit is: He cleanseth it, that it may bear more fruit.

Consider a moment what this pruning or cleansing is. It is not the removal of weeds or thorns or anything from without that may hinder the growth. No; it is the cutting off of the long shoots of the previous year, the removal of something that comes from within, that has been produced by the life of the vine itself. It is the removal of something that is a proof of the vigor of its life; the more vigorous the growth has been, the greater the need for the pruning. It is the honest, healthy wood of the vine that has to be cut away. And why? Because it would consume too much of the sap to fill all the long shoots of last year's growth: the sap must be saved up and used for fruit alone. The branches, sometimes eight and ten feet long, are cut down close to the stem, and nothing is left but just one or two inches of wood, enough to bear the grapes. It is when everything that is not needful for fruit-bearing has been relentlessly cut down, and just as little of the branches as possible has been left, that full, rich fruit may be expected.

What a solemn, precious lesson! It is not to sin only that the cleansing of the Husbandman here refers. It is to our own religious activity, as it is developed in the very act of bearing fruit. It is this that must be cut down and cleansed away. We have, in working for God, to use our natural gifts of wisdom, or eloquence, or influence, or zeal. And yet they are ever in danger of being unduly developed and then trusted in. And so, after each season of work, God has to bring us to the end of ourselves, to the consciousness of the helplessness and the danger of all that is of man, to feel that we are nothing. All that is to be left of us is just enough to receive the power of the life-giving sap of the Holy Spirit. What is of man must be reduced to its very lowest measure. All that is inconsistent with the most entire devotion to Christ's service must be removed. The more perfect the cleansing and cutting away of all that is of self, the less of surface over which the Holy Spirit is to be spread, so much the more intense can be the concentration of our whole being, to be entirely at the disposal of the Spirit. This is the true circumcision of the heart, the circumcision of Christ. This is the true crucifixion with Christ, bearing about the dying of the Lord Jesus in the body.

Blessed cleansing, God's own cleansing! How we may rejoice in the assurance that we shall bring forth more fruit.

-ANDREW MURRAY

Few Love the Cross of Jesus

[Jesus said,] "This people draweth nigh unto me with their mouth, and honoureth me with their lips; but their heart is far from me."

MATTHEW 15:8 KJV

Jesus has always many who love His heavenly kingdom, but few who bear His cross. He has many who desire consolation, but few who care for trial. He finds many to share His table, but few to take part in His fasting. All desire to be happy with Him; few wish to suffer anything for Him. Many follow Him to the breaking of bread, but few to the drinking of the chalice of His passion. Many revere His miracles; few approach the shame of the Cross. Many love Him as long as they encounter no hardship; many praise and bless Him as long as they receive some comfort from Him. But if Jesus hides himself for a while, they fall either into complaints or into deep dejection.

Those, on the contrary, who love Him for His own sake and not for any comfort of their own, bless Him in all trial and anguish of heart as well as in the bliss of consolation. Even if He should never give them consolation, yet they would continue to praise Him and wish always to give Him thanks. What power there is in pure love for Jesus—love that is free from all self-interest and self-love!

Do not those who always seek consolation deserve to be called mercenaries? Do not those who always think of their own profit and gain prove that they love themselves rather than Christ? Where can a man be found who desires to serve God for nothing? Rarely indeed is a man so spiritual as to strip himself of all things. And who shall find a man so truly poor in spirit as to be free from every creature? His value is like that of things brought from the most distant lands.

If a man give all his wealth, it is nothing; if he do great penance, it is little; if he gain all knowledge, he is still far afield; if he have great virtue and much ardent devotion, he still lacks a great deal, and especially, the one thing that is most necessary to him. What is this one thing? That leaving all, he forsake himself, completely renounce himself, and give up all private affections. Then, when he has done all that he knows ought to be done, let him consider it as nothing, let him make little of what may be considered great; let him in all honesty call himself an unprofitable servant. For truth itself has said: "When you shall have done all these things that are commanded you, say: 'we are unprofitable servants.'"

Then he will be truly poor and stripped in spirit, and with the prophet may say: "I am alone and poor."

No one, however, is more wealthy than such a man; no one is more powerful, no one freer than he who knows how to leave all things and think of himself as the least of all.

-THOMAS À KEMPIS

STOP MAKING PROMISES

Peter replied, "Even if all fall away on account of You,
I never will."

MATTHEW 26:33 NIV

To keep the lamp alive
With oil we fill the bowl;
'Tis water makes the willow thrive,
And grace that feeds the soul.
The Lord's unsparing hand
Supplies the living stream
It is not at our own command,
But still derived from him.
Beware of Peter's word,
Nor confidently say,
"I never will deny thee, Lord,"
But grant I never may.
Man's wisdom is to seek
His strength in God alone;
And e'en an angel would be weak,
Who trusted in his own.

-JOHN NEWTON

So often we make promises to God to express our commitment to Him. We say, "I will pray more," or "I will read my Bible more." Yet these promises mean little coming from the mouth of a person who is fallible.

The burden of promise does not lie upon the believer. It is upon God. He is the one who promised to sustain us and give us the ability to live before Him in this world.

If you want to be holy, you must trust in His promise to cleanse you: "If we confess our sins, he is faithful and just to forgive us our sins and to cleanse us from all unrighteousness" (1 John 1:9 KJV).

If you desire to be more diligent in His service, you must trust in His Word to enable you to do so:

"If any man minister, let him do it as of the ability which God giveth: that God in all things may be glorified through Jesus Christ, to whom be praise and dominion for ever and ever. Amen" (1 Peter 4:11 KJV).

We must remember that we can only improve in our lives through trusting in Christ. Only He has the grace to sustain us when we fall short of our—and His—expectations.

BE STILL

The Lord is in his holy temple:
let all the earth keep silence before him.

HABAKKUK 2:20 KJV

Have you ever tried to speak to someone while he or she was still talking to you? With both of your voices going, it was probably very difficult to clearly understand what the other person was saying. But certainly, we have all done this at one time or another, trying to get our point across in the best way possible. True communication comes across most effectively when one is speaking and the other is listening. When both are talking, little is accomplished. This is how our communication with God works also. He listens when we pray. He hears everything we say and brings an answer, if we choose to be still. This is a part of the method of prayer spoken of by Guyon:

We should forget ourselves, and all self-interest, and listen and be attentive to the voice of our God: and these two simple actions, or rather passive dispositions, attract His love to that beauty which He himself communicates.

-MADAME JEANNE GUYON

God wants to say a lot to you today. And one of the most important things you can do in prayer is listen. If you want to hear His voice when you pray, set aside some time to just be quiet in His presence. Listen from your heart rather than your ears. Forget about yourself and concentrate on Him. When you do this, you will begin to hear His voice clearly and will receive all the direction you need. Just be still—be silent before Him and let Him speak.

WITHOUT RESTRAINT

[Jesus said,] "Not what I will, but what thou wilt."

MARK 14:36 KJV

Our love for God can often be expressed by our decision not to fight Him. To lay aside our will in exchange for His perfect desire is one of the most holy occupations in the life of the believer.

Our lives are full of opportunities to fulfill the will of the Father, and it often begins with prayer. It is in the prayer closet that our love connects with the heart of God. This is where we can truly worship Him without restraint. Yet, it is also here where we receive the passion, just as Christ did in Gethsemane, to do the will of the Father, no matter what stands in the way. The Reverend Richard Allen once wrote:

O infinite amiableness! When shall I love thee without bounds, without coldness or interruption which, alas! so often seize me here below? Let me never suffer any creature to be thy rival, or to share my heart with thee; let me have no other God, no other love, but only thee.

-RICHARD ALLEN

Can we share the same convictions? Can our lives reflect the same passion? Yes, and even more so, if we would open up the door of our hearts and allow Him in.

HE WILL CARE FOR
YOUR CARES

[Cast] all your care upon him; for he careth for you.

1 PETER 5:7 KJV

Life can often feel as though it is out of control, and that is just the way God would like it to be. No, God does not want us to walk around feeling helpless. What He does want is for us to begin to live a life that is totally dependent upon Him.

One of the most important things to know as a Christian is that God cares for you. It is this simple truth that helps us to get through our days with the assurance that we are not the ones in control—God is.

[Jesus said,] "Heaven and earth shall pass away: but my words shall not pass away. And take heed to yourselves, lest at any time your hearts be overcharged with surfeiting, and drunkenness, and cares of this life, and so that day come upon you unawares" (Luke 21:33-34 KJV).

"Surfeiting" is the act of feeding yourself excessively with things that can destroy you—clearly, a sin. And we all know that drunkenness has destroyed more families than a few.

However, Jesus equates filling our hearts with the "cares of this life" with two seemingly major sins. Shouldn't we care when bills need to be paid? Shouldn't we care about our businesses and our possessions? Does God expect us to release control of everything?

Releasing our cares upon God is more than just letting go. If we are going to truly let go of our cares, God expects us to cast them upon Him. This way, He can care for our cares. But to do so would require a faith that allows God into the intimate details of our lives. Do we dare hesitate at such an admonition to "cast our cares upon Him"? Is He not our Savior? If we cannot cast our cares upon Him, then what is He really the Savior of in our lives?

Jesus is not only the Savior that delivers us from hell, but also from sickness, lack, and anything that would attempt to hold us back from living a life of abundance. Jesus spilled His blood on the cross so that we would not have to ever be comfortless in this world. He is an ever-present help in times of trouble. But He will not take the passenger seat. He wants to drive your life into the destination that He wants to go—the place that is best for you. He wants you to let Him into your life and give Him everything. And once you do that, nothing is going to be withheld from you.

Is life out of control? Step aside and let the Master care for your cares. As He does, you can find refuge at His right hand, in the passenger seat, and cheer Him on. You can offer Him all the praise He deserves. He is going to take you to a life unforgettable, unmatchable, with joy unspeakable!

Priceless Treasure

[Jesus said,] "Where your treasure is, there will your heart be also."

Matthew 6:21 kjv

Expeditions from all over the country rushed to California during the 1800s, looking to find gold in the city of Sacramento. Some spent their life's savings just for the trip. They sought wealth and riches. They sought fame and power. But the thing that would bring all of those great worldly attributes was gold. But instead of gold, many found death and sickness. Many found violence and struggle. Yet, even in struggle, many found the gold which they sought. Yes, there were many who had a motive of greed. But their hearts were in the treasure they sought, and nothing could stop them from finding it.

Many people spend too much of their lives trying to find their treasure. And even though there is no modernday gold rush in Sacramento, there is a gold rush. All people want perfection. They want riches. They want to lose weight. They want to get a better education. They want to be happy. But in their search, the happiness never comes because you can never truly find your heart through the things of this world.

How many people search far and wide to find their hearts? How many years go by, with Christians all over the world vainly trying to find their hearts in the things of this world? It cannot be done.

The true treasure is a relationship with God. It is a love walk towards Him that causes a person to find his or her heart. Once the heart is found, there is no longer a need to search for treasure anywhere else. Jesus will be our treasure and will abide in our hearts, which shall be His home.

PREPARATION

Eye hath not seen, nor ear heard, neither have entered into the heart of man, the things which God hath prepared for them that love him.

1 CORINTHIANS 2:9 KJV

Once dubbed as the fastest man on the planet, Jesse Owens spent his life in preparation for his moment in the 1936 Olympics. That year, Adolph Hitler was set to prove that the German "Aryan" people were superior. By the end of the competition, even the Aryan people of Germany were cheering for the American athlete, Jesse Owens. Owens triumphed that year, and from then on he lived a distinguished life, being loved and respected the world over.

"A lifetime of training for just ten seconds," said Owens, remembering his triumph. How right he was.

We live a lifetime of trials, tribulations, and challenges that, at times, stretch our willingness to continue in our walk with God. Hardships can at times make us wonder whether or not it is worth it to continue in our walk. But when we think of Jesse Owens running along a dirt road without anyone looking; when we think back at his poverty-stricken upbringing; when we look at the sacrifices he had to endure in his life for a race that lasted mere seconds, we must conclude that our lives also are a preparation for a moment of greatness.

And only you will know it when that moment comes. In 1937, Jesse Owens proved Hitler wrong by running a race that everyone thought he would lose. His preparation paid off.

There are great things ahead for you. But will you, in obscurity, remain faithful to God through the issues of life? Will you be prepared when the time comes?

TEMPTATION

*There hath no temptation taken you but such as is common to man:
but God is faithful, who will not suffer you to be tempted above that
ye are able; but will with the temptation also make a way to escape,
that ye may be able to bear it.*

1 CORINTHIANS 10:13 KJV

So long as we live in this world we cannot escape suffering
and temptation. Whence it is written in Job: "The life of man
upon earth is a warfare." Everyone, therefore, must guard
against temptation and must watch in prayer lest the devil,
who never sleeps but goes about seeking whom he may
devour, find occasion to deceive him. No one is so perfect or
so holy but he is sometimes tempted; man cannot be altogeth-
er free from temptation.

Yet temptations, though troublesome and severe, are often
useful to a man, for in them he is humbled, purified, and
instructed. The saints all passed through many temptations
and trials to profit by them, while those who could not resist
became reprobate and fell away. There is no state so holy, no
place so secret that temptations and trials will not come. Man
is never safe from them as long as he lives, for they come from
within us—in sin we were born. When one temptation or
trial passes, another comes; we shall always have something to
suffer because we have lost the state of original blessedness.

Many people try to escape temptations, only to fall more deeply. We cannot conquer simply by fleeing, but by patience and true humility we become stronger than all our enemies. The man who only shuns temptations outwardly and does not uproot them will make little progress; indeed they will quickly return, more violent than before.

Little by little, in patience and long-suffering you will overcome them, by the help of God rather than by severity and your own rash ways. Often take counsel when tempted; and do not be harsh with others who are tempted, but console them as you yourself would wish to be consoled.

The beginning of all temptation lies in a wavering mind and little trust in God, for as a rudderless ship is driven hither and yon by waves, so a careless and irresolute man is tempted in many ways. Fire tempers iron, and temptation steels the just. Often we do not know what we can stand, but temptation shows us what we are.

Above all, we must be especially alert against the beginnings of temptation, for the enemy is more easily conquered if he is refused admittance to the mind and is met beyond the threshold when he knocks.

Someone has said very aptly: "Resist the beginnings; remedies come too late, when by long delay the evil has gained strength." First, a mere thought comes to mind, then strong imagination, followed by pleasure, evil delight, and consent. Thus, because he is not resisted in the beginning, Satan gains full entry. And the longer a man delays in resisting, so much the weaker does he become each day, while the strength of the enemy grows against him.

Some suffer great temptations in the beginning of their conversion, others toward the end, while some are troubled almost constantly throughout their life. Others, again, are tempted but lightly according to the wisdom and justice of Divine Providence who weighs the status and merit of each and prepares all for the salvation of His elect.

We should not despair, therefore, when we are tempted, but pray to God the more fervently that He may see fit to help us, for according to the word of Paul, He will make issue with temptation that we may be able to bear it. Let us humble our souls under the hand of God in every trial and temptation, for He will save and exalt the humble in spirit.

In temptations and trials the progress of a man is measured; in them opportunity for merit and virtue is made more manifest.

When a man is not troubled it is not hard for him to be fervent and devout, but if he bears up patiently in time of adversity, there is hope for great progress.

Some, guarded against great temptations, are frequently overcome by small ones in order that, humbled by their weakness in small trials, they may not presume on their own strength in great ones.

-THOMAS À KEMPIS
THE IMITATION OF CHRIST

THE METHOD OF PRAYER

Be careful for nothing; but in every thing by prayer and supplication
with thanksgiving let your requests be made known unto God.

PHILIPPIANS 4:6 KJV

There are two ways of introducing a soul into prayer, which should for some time be pursued; the one is Meditation, the other is Reading accompanied with Meditation.

Meditative Reading is the choosing of some important practical or speculative truth, always preferring the practical, and proceeding thus: whatever truth you have chosen, read only a small portion of it, endeavoring to taste and digest it, to extract the essence and substance thereof, and proceed no farther while any savor or relish remains in the passage: when this subsides, take up your book again and proceed as before, seldom reading more than half a page at a time, for it is not the quantity that is read, but the manner of reading, that yields us profit.

Those who read fast reap no more advantage than a bee would by only skimming over the surface of the flower, instead of waiting to penetrate into it, and extract its sweets. Much reading is rather for scholastic subjects than divine truths: indeed, to receive real profit from spiritual books, we must read as I have described; and I am certain, if that method were pursued, we should become gradually habituated to, and more fully disposed for prayer.

Meditation, which is the other method, is to be practiced at an appropriated season, and not in the time of reading. I believe the best manner of meditating is as follows: When by an act of lively faith, you are placed in the Presence of God, recollect some truth wherein there is substance and food; pause gently and sweetly thereon, not to employ the reason, but merely to calm and fix the mind: for you must observe, that your principal exercise should ever be the Presence of God; your subject, therefore, should rather serve to stay the mind, than exercise the understanding.

From this procedure, it will necessarily follow, that the lively faith in a God immediately present in our inmost soul, will produce an eager and vehement pressing inwardly into ourselves, and a restraining all our senses from wandering abroad: this serves to extricate us speedily from numberless distractions, to remove us far from external objects, and to bring us nigh unto our God, who is only to be found in our inmost centre, which is the Holy of Holies wherein He dwelleth.

-MADAME JEANNE GUYON

Additional copies of this and
other Honor Books products are available
wherever good books are sold.

Water From the Rock: Classic Edition
Water From the Rock: Meditations on Peace and Purpose
Water From the Rock: Meditations on Grace and Hope

❖ ❖ ❖

If you have enjoyed this book,
or if it has had an impact on your life,
we would like to hear from you.

Please contact us at:

HONOR BOOKS
Cook Communications Ministries, Dept. 201
4050 Lee Vance View
Colorado Springs, CO 80918
Or visit our Web site:
www.cookministries.com

HONORBOOKS

Inspiration and Motivation for the Season of Life